W9-CVA-733

MYSTERY
AND
MEANING

MYSTERY
AND
MEANING

PERSONAL LOGIC
AND THE LANGUAGE OF RELIGION

BY
DOUGLAS A. FOX

THE WESTMINSTER PRESS

PHILADELPHIA

Copyright © 1975 The Westminster Press

Book Design by Dorothy Alden Smith

Published by The Westminster Press ®
Philadelphia, Pennsylvania

PRINTED IN THE UNITED STATES OF AMERICA

Library of Congress Cataloging in Publication Data

Fox, Douglas A   1927–
    Mystery and meaning.

    Includes bibliographical references.
    1. Theology. I. Title.
    BR118.F74   201'.1   75–15738
    ISBN 0–664–24768–7

For Elizabeth and Michael

Contents

(continued on next page)

Acknowledgments

It is a pleasant duty to acknowledge with love and very deep gratitude the patient endurance of my wife, Margaret, and my children, Elizabeth and Michael, who orbited around in circumspect good humor while this book was being written. In addition to them, the list of persons who have contributed something to it would be endless and must include former teachers who have impressed, illumined, or disgusted me. Among these (although *never* occasioning disgust!) the foremost is Professor Wayne R. Rood of the Pacific School of Religion, who drew my attention to the ideas of John Macmurray and guided me through the rigors of a doctoral program in which Macmurray's embryonic dialogical form figured prominently.

I am grateful, too, to the administration and trustees of The Colorado College for affording a sabbatical leave during which the work could be completed. And to my colleagues in the Religion Department of that college, for failing to detect my absence.

A
Word
to
Begin

Many years ago, after enthusiastically dropping out of high school, I spent several discouraging months as a filing clerk in a small but busy office. The job should have been dull routine, but my predecessor had taken care of that. Having grown tired of inserting things in files and, upon request, taking them out again, he simply gave up filing anything. He allowed a huge pile of letters, contracts, memos, and other material to accumulate in a corner of the office while he used his time to read, to hunt frenziedly for anything that had been requested, and to seek more congenial employment.

Inevitably his neglect was one day detected and he was instructed to get everything in order within a week or face dismissal. He did not want to leave just yet, but neither did he want to undertake the monumental task of catching up with the filing, so he devised an ingenious alternative: he simply opened files at random and inserted a handful of assorted material without the least concern for the relevance of the file to the matter entering it.

How long this went on I do not know. But when I took over the filing room its files were in a state of splendid chaos, each one a mass of unrelated data.

The mind of many a Christian is, at least in regard to his religious ideas, very much like my files. He has a history of having occasionally spurred himself to more or less serious reading of the Bible or of books that massively oversimplify the Faith; he has a record of sporadic Sunday school attendance; he goes to church once in a while. But from all this he has garnered a curious and exotic kaleidoscope of unorganized pieces of information and, alas, misinformation. He has the names of a few Biblical books, half the Twenty-third Psalm, a smattering of Jewish and Christian legend and history marvelously intertwined, and a confusion of patriarchs. What he lacks is not only an organized memory but any useful key that might enable him to walk through the wayward weeds of his intellectual garden and select an acceptable bouquet.

Nor is this problem exclusive to Christian *laymen.* One result of some lamentable traditions in theological education is a clergy whose minds are little better organized, even in respect of theology, than those of their congregation. Of course they know a great deal more, and what they know is usually both more accurate and more profound. But since they learned their systematic theology as one subject, pastoral psychology as another, church history, sociology of religion, Biblical languages, liturgiology, religious education, and Old and New Testament exegesis all as separate "subjects," separate virginal bodies to be protected from intercourse at all costs, they are often as lacking in ordered understanding as anyone could be.

In short, I am afraid that most of us who think of ourselves as Christians, whether layman or cleric, fail to have or to use any tool or method for achieving clarity in our thinking about our commitments and beliefs.

This is serious. Not only does it mean that we continue to live with confusion, but we cannot competently give "a reason of the hope that is in us" or talk with anyone in a way that makes apparent the astonishing relevance of Christianity for today's world. It is not just that we need to know more theology or philosophy or psychology or something, but that we need to discover how to order our thinking so that the various facets of our understanding can have a mutually critical and enriching engagement. We need to be able to see ways in which things we believe fit together and, consequently, to see when they fail to do so.

It is one purpose of this book to try to suggest a way of viewing Christian thought that will bring some order as well as some critical and constructive thrust to our thinking.

Systems, however, can be deadly. Karl Rahner has said that ours is not a time for a *summa,* for a comprehensive systematic theology, but for explorations. With this I agree, yet explorations that do not proceed systematically are likely to resemble the expeditions of luckless adventurers who have wandered into the deserts of Australia or the forests of America never to be heard of again. Our need, then, is for a means of systematic thinking that does not lead to rigidity and the closing of minds to further possibilities, and we here present dialogical theology as precisely such an instrument. It is a tool for putting some ideas together and for opening up certain areas of meaning. But it is not the necessary and sufficient instrument of Christian theology. It can help us to see and to say some things that are illuminating, and it may be (as I believe) uniquely faithful to the structure of the foundational experiences of Christianity, but it cannot possibly uncover all that Christian faith intends, and its own dialogical character precludes our accepting it as if it were a solitary and sufficient voice.

We are to be concerned in the following pages, then, with an orderly approach to Christian ideas. And we are concerned to try to bridge the increasing intellectual gulf between the professional theologian and the layman, for this gulf is creating two Christian communities among us with almost no useful communication between them.

Theologians tend to write for theologians; they are consequently ignored by laymen who suspect that much of the difficulty in theological language is unnecessary and is a sort of status symbol prized by those who think themselves the church's intellectual elite. To make matters worse, thoughtful laymen are often a little doubtful about those theologians who do write intelligible books—are they the cop-outs of their community? Were they unable to make it in the thin air of the professional? Have they distorted the truth in their quest for popularity or can they, indeed, make it "popular" because they are luckless enough not to understand it properly themselves? In many cases, of course, the popularizer is too patently guilty of patronizing his public, of "talking down" to his audience, so that his book, though widely read, provokes a strange resistance.

The present book may certainly fail in what it undertakes. But it is hoped that the following pages will be intelligible to the amateur as well as the professional theologian and, in making a contribution to the continuous task of constructive theology, will stimulate productive thought for laity and clergy alike. This means that the latter will sometimes have to endure explanations that they do not need. On the other hand, I can make no pretense of being able to discuss the issues contained in this work in a way that is sure to be perfectly limpid to someone who has no acquaintance with philosophy or theology—not even a college course or two, or the experience of having read an introduction to one of these subjects that provided guidance for handling philosophical terms and methods. Even without this preparation, however, I trust that many will find that patience—a willingness to read slowly and to fight every inch of the way—will suffice to break open the book's meaning.

The content of this work is designed to achieve certain specific goals other than those general intentions already mentioned.

First, we hope to indicate the most appropriate structure of apprehension for Christianity. Frederick J. Streng, in his book *Emptiness: A Study in Religious Meaning* (Abingdon Press, 1967), has lucidly described three "structures of religious apprehension" between which he evidently believes we can divide the world's religious traditions. These are the "mythical," "intuitional," and "dialectic"—the latter having a special reference to the second-century Buddhist philosopher Nagarjuna and his followers. Streng makes the point, largely valid I believe, that there is a sort of cultural "structure of apprehension," closely related to language, which sets the limits and largely determines the form of our religious experience and our interpretation of it.

I believe that Christianity makes use of all the modes of religious understanding discussed by Streng, but that we have tended to overlook one other mode—and that the most important of them all. It is my contention in this book that the "new wine" with which Christianity burst the old religious and cultural wineskins of its milieu was what we shall be calling a "dialogical" mode of apprehension. The fact that for two thousand years we have tended to be satisfied with mythical, intuitional, and dialectical substitutes for dialogical thought and experience (but more often for the thought than the experience) means—no less—that we have kept replacing the vanquished wineskins with others of their kind and, consequently, have failed to recognize the dynamic of the new wine.

Again, the present book accepts the responsibility of standing against the stream of contemporary fascinations, at least in certain selected respects. Sam Keen and others have urged that we need today a Dionysian theology—that is, one characterized by a sense of divine immanence, by a mood of fire and dance. And we are confronted by a plethora of books and essays that spring from the busy loins of contemporary Jesus romanticism. Jesus, we are told, is not "coming again," because he has never left us; he is alive within us. True enough, of course, but only half the message of the New Testament and consequently a great misrepresentation of even that half. Indeed, one may feel a little alarm at all this, because romanticism, however it releases our inhibitions and satisfies long concealed longings, however it liberates us in nights of moonlit intoxication, tends so often to leave us merely embarrassed when we awaken again to a reasonable morning.

Alas, almost all attempts to write theology of a fine Dionysian madness seem to degenerate sadly into forays toward something like simple silliness: he who is drunk rarely appears splendid to him who is sober, and while occasional dizziness is a satisfying corrective to dull sobriety, it can hardly stand as a way of life.

Yet it is true that staid Apollo needs dancing Dionysus; and vice versa. So the present work tries to find a way of integrating the spirits of both so that neither, in murdering his brother, is left alone to suffer his inevitable remorse and eventual suicide. Indeed, dialogical theology seems to me precisely the happy union of Apollo and Dionysus. But that is a metaphor we had better, perhaps, leave undeveloped.

Again, ours is a time of many theological experiments, some of which seem to me to propose pathways that miss Christianity altogether. In some quarters it is said, for example, that the classical affirmation that Jesus is the Christ is no part of the "real" truth about him; that he did not understand himself in such terms, and that the staunch defense of his Christhood in the New Testament is an invention not only of Christians but of *Gentile* Christians evidently attempting a sort of one-upmanship at the expense of their Jewish associates. Jesus, instead, is a teacher of ethics the heart of whose message is simply "Repent!"

Against such trends we shall argue that Christology is the most urgent business on the current theological agenda. The crucial question for all of us is still that which Jesus is supposed to have asked his friends: "Who do you say that I am?" (Matt. 16:15). If, with Peter, we answer "The Christ!" we do not merely make a statement about the function of Jesus but we open for ourselves a unique way of understanding reality itself. Indeed, the present work will try to indicate why any retreat from Christological claims for Jesus is not only unnecessary but a shallow abandonment of a magnificently luminous world view.

We shall dare to say that Jesus is of critical contemporary importance *as the Christ*, whether he thought of himself in that fashion or not!

Penultimately, the following pages try to recover the wonder and the importance of two related elements of our experience that philosophy and theology are often tempted to disvalue and that some religious traditions actually deny: the personal character of authentic human existence, and what we shall call "otherness." The latter may need a word of preliminary explanation.

When I was a young man I left my homeland to find, if I could, a deeper, larger truth about life. What I have learned is that I need not have neglected or abandoned the simplest and most immediate experiences that come to us. I can remember now a long, white set of wooden steps rising from a bay shore to the top of a very steep hill, and beside and underneath it, thrusting out from the moist earth, a hundred nameless (nameless to me) weeds and flowers. If one day I had stopped halfway up those steps to spend an hour with one green finger of life, if I had thought about its meaning, I would have discovered something that eluded me for years: that the first fact of our awakening to life is otherness: the otherness of persons, certainly, but also of the smallest and simplest things.

Otherness awakens us to our own finitude. We are, consequently, constrained to ignore it if we can. If we cannot ignore it, we erect vast systems of philosophy or of mysticism to transcend it, to obliterate it, to render it meaningless. But otherness returns to haunt us. The mystic who knows his moment of undifferentiated oneness must find again the world he has discarded and live in it—or, rather, it finds him and demands that he make concessions to it or die (which dilemma he usually settles by making a carefully rationalized concession). Otherness raises questions about the meaning of my existence, about my endurance, my limits. But we ignore otherness only by what is finally an act of will and also, I think, an act of bad faith toward life. We ignore it by refusing to begin our understanding of ourselves with the first datum of experience.

So "otherness" finds its place in our thinking here, and so does personhood (which cannot exist without otherness).

Finally we are trying here to put theology in its proper place: a noble enough place, but a humbler one than that to which it sometimes aspires. Theology is a very funny business, especially when it is pursued by unreservedly serious men. Indeed, one of the more remarkable symptoms of ineffectual spirituality is the deadly and earnest pedantry that so often attends the craft of theology.

After all, theology is properly an intellectual caboose, coming when the exciting part of the train has passed. But unhappily, by a kind of demonic magic, it too often manages to derail the train and roll along in solitary possession of the track. No one, except perhaps Mani, ever deliberately invented a religion by first proposing a theological system. The usual sequence is *first* an intense experience or awareness of what is held to be a living truth (not conceptualized yet) that somehow invades or impinges upon our life. It is an experience that evokes response, decision, and action, and that finally stimulates reflection of a more or less systematic kind.

Next, a tradition arises around the initial experience, limpingly trying to describe it, indicate it, or at least invite to it, and this tradition is far less important, at first, in its ideological or behavioral details than in the manner in which it indicates the possibility of renewing the experience itself. But in the course of composing the tradition we try to say something about the Great Reality that is the source and/or power and meaning of the initial experience. At this point, however unwillingly or unwittingly, we betray some of our philosophical assumptions by what we affirm and what we deny, and soon—pitifully soon—the cluster of ideas we have used as tools of communication become petards with which to hoist our enemy, and standards of unequivocal orthodoxy for ourselves. Words and ideas have superseded the encounter with Reality, with God. And theology has become a respectable profession.

Of course, exceptional figures arise occasionally to prick the bubble of our priggishness. Søren Kierkegaard, despite his gloom, was such a man, and it is hard to see how theology could ever have been the same after him. But it is. In fact, it is more the same than ever. Yet what Kierkegaard saw is the eternal spear stuck in the guts of any of us who make our living by peddling religious sentences. He saw that the initial experience of Christianity is the absurd intrusion of the Eternal into our time, of the Spaceless into our space—an intrusion that demands subjective response, that calls for the commitment of faith. He saw (as, curiously, Zen is reminding some of us today) that reason has to be broken open before the perception of Ultimacy can be born, or it purveys only a glittering parody. To understand this is not to abandon theology, but to become aware of its limits.

It is important that the limited nature and function of theology be remembered. Otherwise that which theology ought to serve (the direct encounter of persons with each other and with the God in whom they all exist) will be lost. Carter Dickson, in *The Magic Lantern Murders*,[1] says:

> It has been remarked that poets do not go mad, but mathematicians do. The poet only wishes to get his head into the heavens. It is the scientist who wishes to get the heavens into his head: and it is his head which splits.

Theologians who have no sense of the limit of their craft —and no sense of humor—are worse than scientists.

PART ONE

THE
CONTEXT
OF
THEOLOGY

CHAPTER 2

The
Christian
Tradition

Religion is as common as calamity and as indefinable as poetry. It is derided, abandoned, and abused, yet it persists in such a variety of forms and moods that no reasonable discussion of human affairs can for long ignore it. But what is it?

If religion entails belief in God or gods, Buddhism in some of its forms is not religious. If religion must include the cultivation of disciplines in which men try to reach and merge with some infinite reality, Christians who believe that the infinite God has already embraced men, making such disciplines unnecessary, are irreligious. If religion requires a belief in some absolutely transcendent reality, many forms of piety must be set aside because they hold that truth and reality are within us. In fact, despite dozens of attempts, no definition or description of religion has ever proved universally satisfying. Yet there are few who would not say that there is *something* that is religious and that this is in some way different from whatever is purely philosophical, ethical, political, or aesthetic.

The difficulty of defining religion leads many pious or impious persons to be content with incredibly ill-assorted ideas on the subject, the assumption seeming to be either that orderly thinking would destroy the delicate blossom, or that religion is but a dandelion upon which the rigor of hard thought need not be wasted.

This intellectual carelessness is unfortunate. It robs the unreligious person of a chance to understand the surprising power and persistence of a phenomenon that has achieved more in human history than it is possible to calculate. And it reduces the devout to an incoherence that may not only make it hard for them to speak intelligibly about what moves them but that may also make them vulnerable to all manner of distortions of the religious impulse.

What, then, is at the heart of whatever we call "religious"? I would like to suggest that when we penetrate to the center of religion we find there a sense of an immediate apprehension of something—some truth or reality—which illuminates the whole of existence, giving profound value to our life and endowing it, or some manner of living it, with a satisfying sense of meaningfulness. I am not suggesting that every participant in a religious tradition has himself experienced this apprehension, but only that at the center of the religious tradition itself this apprehension can be found.

To have the sort of experience I am describing is sometimes like finding the key piece to a jigsaw puzzle, or like having one's surroundings suddenly illuminated by a flash of lightning. It is not that one has grasped a proposition about life that feels true; rather, one has perceived a meaning or reality beyond all propositions, in the light of which one begins to feel at home in the universe. As a result of this experience one may begin to say many things about life, but the experience is something that cannot itself be adequately reduced to words. It is the experience of a Buddha as he sits beneath a tree and is awakened to the law of causation which binds the process of the universe, and to all the suprarational concomitants of that law. It is the experience of the disciples of Jesus as they huddle obscurely in an upper room and feel themselves overwhelmed by God's presence until they are driven out to preach their new understanding of the Christhood of their former friend and leader. It is the experience of Zarathustra as he prayerfully begs understanding of why there is a universe and feels himself met by God's presence; Shankara's discovery of Brahman, Israel's covenanting encounter with Yahweh at Sinai, and a Taoist's knowing of the Tao are all instances of this experience of apprehension.

Thus, while "religion" eludes definition, we can say that any enduring religious tradition must begin in the kind of experience we have been discussing—an intuitive, immediate, illuminating awareness. This vision is not experienced as the calmly received end of a train of logical inquiry, but is felt as a liberating and supralogical "arrival." To have it is to feel oneself "born again" or "awakened" to new and decisive perspectives. The qualities of intuitive immediacy and of unique personal liberation and renewal are what seem most commonly to distinguish a religious from a simply philosophical tradition, although religion begets philosophy, and philosophy may occasionally provoke the religious kind and degree of apprehension.

But let us try to isolate a little more clearly the distinctive character of the religious awakening.

Natural sciences and many philosophies explore the universe in order to discover and, perhaps, to exploit its order. They ask what is the connection between certain kinds of events, what are the constituent elements in things, how have things come to be as they are, and so on. Empirical observation and orderly reasoning are the tools by which these inquiries proceed.

If, however, one goes farther to ask why there is a universe to study, why there is something instead of nothing, he is likely to be told that this is an unanswerable and therefore unprofitable question; even, perhaps, that it is meaningless. Of those who respond in this way Joseph Sittler remarks, "They should not be surprised that many in our time who retain a primal curiosity about total-meaning, dismiss their dismissal as a perilous sickness."[2]

Even when someone goes beyond science to ask the question about what Sittler calls "total-meaning" he may try to satisfy himself with an entirely rational answer, moving from premise to conclusion with no "leaps" or incongruities and accepting as premise only what seems to him inescapable. But it is also possible that he may one day find himself grasped by a perception of total-meaning that seems to have reached him from somewhere outside the series of steps his reason has taken. It may not be in conflict with reason, but it is a "truth" that he will feel to have grasped him rather than to have been grasped by him. The philosopher is enthusiastic about a "position" he can defend, but the man we are discussing is the devotee of some thing or some One in defense of which no possible words are entirely appropriate.

A man may entertain a point of view with a high degree of detachment, or he may have a sense of loyalty to something he knows perfectly well is itself frail and limited. But *religious traditions begin after one or more persons find themselves drawn into a loyalty, a total commitment of themselves, to an object of devotion that touches all their life and world with at least the hope of meaning.*

This moment of awakening and commitment, this new vision and this dawning of truth constitute what we shall call the Central Generating Experience of religion.

Christianity stems from a distinctive experience: an awakening to the Christhood of Jesus, together with all that this means for the world in which he has appeared. It will be the contention of this book that this Christian Central Generating Experience remains uniquely luminous, opening the minds that receive it to an unsurpassed vision of life.

Before we proceed to try, with futile sentences, to indicate the meaning of the central Christian experience (that is, to think theologically), it may preserve our perspective if we consider briefly the complex structure of Christianity as a tradition and the place in it of our present enterprise—theology. We shall then be warned that even to have a perceptive theology of supreme excellence is to do no more than touch the fringe of the rich and ripe tradition of our faith.

The Structure
of a Religious Tradition

The first instance of a Generating Experience is not necessarily the beginning of a great tradition. The ecstasy of the disciples in their upper room may be, as some like to say, the birth of the church, but the church would have been stillborn if things had gone no farther than that. For a luminous moment of awakening, a Central Generating Experience, to promote a religious tradition such as the Christian it is necessary that those who have had the vision allow it to confront their environment of persons, structures, and orders of nature. The question must be asked, What does it mean that this has happened to us in such a world as this? A world in which there is disease and disorder as well as joy and health? In which suspicion and trust, cruelty and kindness coexist? In which there are rich men and poor, fools and sages, mountains, valleys, rivers, clouds, grass, and grains of dirt?

As men allow their central religious experience to question and be questioned by their environment, and as they attempt to express the meaning of what they have seen to and for that environment, a tradition emerges that grows more elaborate as the generations pass, and that finally contains at least five major segments, as shown in our diagram.

We have said that the Generating Experience of a religious tradition is felt to sunder the limits of pure reason. Human beings, however, are beings endowed with reason, and they cannot be fulfilled by its neglect. So they cannot resist trying to order and explicate their experiences—to make "sense" of what has happened to them and what they feel—and when an experience is compelling enough they want to communicate it. It is thus that the items within the category we have called "intellectualization" are born from the womb of religious awakening. Theology and philosophy begin as the attempts to make clear what can be said, indeed what *must* be said, after the awakening, to pursue implications, to discuss the meaning of the generative event for the world and of the world for that event. They use whatever language, whatever concepts are available, and they may even invent a few. But to the end these

CENTRAL GENERATING EXPERIENCE

THE ENVIRONMENT

in interaction with

produces a

CUMULATIVE TRADITION

containing

INTELLECT-UALIZATION	CHARACTER CONCERN	RE-PRESENTATION	SECONDARY SUPPORTIVE EMOTIONS	COMMUNITY
Philosophy	Ethics	Myth	Stimulated enthusiasm	Church
Theology	Morality	Ritual	Sentiment	Religious group or tribe
Apologetics	Norms and ideals		Loyalty	
Proclamation	Disciplines		Preliminary mystical states	
Science	Concepts of sainthood		Aesthetic experience	
Educational theory	Educating		Celebration	

remain at a loss to do complete justice to what has been intuitively perceived.

Sooner or later the religious person will begin to defend his point of view against misrepresentation and attack; he will try to find better ways to recommend it, and he will point out as effectively as he can that the original generative experience is but the paradigm of one that others may have. Here begin apologetics and proclamation, and these may take many forms: preaching, poetry, drama, novel, closely reasoned argument, or even attempts to construct a system of education or a program of conditioning.

In a tradition that takes the world seriously it may not be long before science also arises as a feature of the intellectual life of those who have shared the same kind of generative experience. The tools of science, especially social science, will be used to study and evaluate the tradition and its influence, and the scientific analysis of religion may at last become a specialized academic discipline. In addition, persons of religious commitment may use perspectives provided by their faith as hypotheses for the scientific examination and interpretation of data in general, as the celebrated Jesuit paleontologist Pierre Teilhard de Chardin did so intriguingly.

Thus there comes into existence a body of thought designed to explore, understand, and express the significance not only of the original generative moment but also of its products. The philosophy contained herein includes the critical analysis of itself as well as attempts to make constructive statements that will disclose the meaning and value structures that the central experience seems to suggest. This philosophy will include language analysis, metaphysics, epistemology,

and, indeed, the entire range of philosophical possibilities, but it will be devoted to a content circumscribed
by its point of origin, the Central Generating Experience and the consequent religious tradition.

Originally the main purpose for all this intellectual
activity is probably to celebrate the dynamic generative experience and to recommend it, making clear
the fact that such an experience is not simply a once-
occurring thing of importance only as a cultic memory,
but that it is a live possibility for any normal person
either in this or in some future time for which he must
prepare now. There will eventually be some study of
the conditions that seem to favor the recapturing of the
experience, and from such interests the psychology of
religion will become a more or less respectable schol-
arly enterprise.

In time, of course, the intellectualizing tends to become an end in itself and is done by people who have
no personal interest in enjoying the generative experience and thus themselves becoming an enraptured dis-
ciple of Jesus or a Buddha or a religious enthusiast of
any sort.

In addition to the activities we have discussed, there
are those listed in our diagram under the heading
"Character Concern." Someone begins to ask about the
kind of behavior appropriate for those who have had or
who earnestly hope to have the generative experience:
when you have been, or wish to be, encountered by
God, what do you do? So we find ethics, systems and
rules of morality, ideals, and forms of discipline taking
shape, and there emerges some image of the ideal person, the saint. At first the end sought in all this is rarely
either sainthood or moral perfection for its own sake;
rather it is the recovery and extension of the generative

experience. Either a person must live according to an ethic, for instance, in order to achieve salvation, or the hope and experience of salvation imply some sort of ethic. In any case, behavioral expectations and a character-ideal arise in association with the developing tradition.

Another common element in religious traditions is the re-presentation of events surrounding, precipitating, or supporting the original instance of the Central Generating Experience. So stories are told about the great focal figures—Jesus, Muhammad, the Buddha—or about great legendary participants in the tradition, such as Krishna, Rama, Paul, Abu Bekr, and so on. These stories are the myths of the faith. Of course it must be pointed out as forcefully as possible that to call these stories "myths" does not imply that they are untrue. A myth is by no means a fairy tale or mere fantasy. It is a story about things of ultimate and even supramundane value couched in the terms and experiences of this world, and it may very well be a perfectly accurate account of events that really happened. What makes the story of the crucifixion of Jesus a Christian myth is not its truth or falsity in terms of historical fact but its *function* in the continuing Christian tradition. Christians see in it something more than the simple story of a tragic death. It is symbolic of the interaction of God and the world, and therefore it is properly termed a myth.

So myth arises as the re-presentation of the events surrounding and including the first awakening at the heart of the tradition. The stories are told over and over in the hope that they will create a context for the recovery of the generative experience itself.

Similarly, ritual arises as re-presentation. When

Christians celebrate the Eucharist or Holy Communion they enact the story of the famous "last supper" shared by Jesus and his disciples. The purpose of doing this is, above all, to reproduce an important element in the context of the pristine generative experience—the awakening of the disciples to the Christhood (the God-for-us-ness) of Jesus.

I do not wish to labor this explication of our diagram, and I think that little needs to be said about the last two sections. As means to the end desired—the recovery of the Central Generating Experience—many religious bodies quite deliberately cultivate in their adherents emotional responses that support in some way the main quest. Thus the contemporary survivals of American frontier religion make great use of the aroused enthusiasm of the revivalist meeting. Buddhists cultivate certain "preliminary" mystical states on the way to the ultimate awakening they seek. Loyalty to a church or to the tradition itself; celebration of the fact or the possibility of the central experience or of events and persons who somehow support it; and the stimulation of aesthetic responses to art that points toward or serves the religious awakening—all these are "secondary supportive emotions." These emotions may be freely used and, incidentally, may sometimes become so satisfying that they supplant the original goal itself. Many a person who enjoys the stimulation of a rousing hymn would be quite dismayed to have to awaken to the actual presence of God!

Finally, a religious tradition creates a community of common interest, common vision, common hope.

It is doubtful whether anyone ever makes use of all the elements available to him in the tradition to which he belongs. There are Christians who are preoccupied with what they take to be Christian morality, but know nothing about theology and are unenthusiastic about ritual or the church. Others love to involve themselves in the discussion of theology or philosophy but express in their lives moral values that would discredit a rabbit. In the pages that follow we shall certainly be selective in our interest, most of our thought falling into the categories of philosophy, character concern and, especially, theology; but it is useful for us to see where our present interests fit into the much wider arena of Christianity, lest we think we are exhausting all the dimensions of the faith. There are more things in the Christian heaven and earth than shall be dreamed of in our philosophy.

CHAPTER 3

Thinking About the Unthinkable

God is unthinkable. He is beyond imagining, conceptualizing, or grasping by any of our intellectual tools. This is a basic conviction of Christian theology and has to be taken seriously, because if it is not, our discussion of God soon degenerates into an absurd anthropomorphism in which he becomes remarkably like us. It is God's privilege, if he chooses, to make us in *his* image (whatever that means), but it is never ours to return the compliment.

Yet God impinges, at least potentially, upon the experience of anyone. God is the being—the "is-ness"—of whatever is, and he touches us whenever we break through the dull acceptance of our customary attitudes to sense the impenetrable mystery of Being, the wonder of the fact that there is something rather than nothing. This is not to reduce God to existence or to say that our existence somehow proves the existence or reality of God, for the God of whom Christians speak simply could not be proven to exist without being destroyed. To prove that an entity exists is to make it a part of some order of meaning or of being on which it depends or which depends on it, and, in either case, it is to reduce it to the status of inclusion in a larger whole. God is not a part of anything, but is that Whole in which everything finds itself; consequently God cannot be "proven."

The experience of God's presence is in part or at times the experience we have of the wonder of Being, including our wonder at the being of particularity, of difference, of personal identity and otherness. And when certain events become transparent to the presence of God, the ultimately real Being itself, in such a way that we are grasped by a meaning in them that points to supreme value, we encounter God in a way that modifies our response to him and gives theology something new to say. Thus, when Christians wonderingly discovered that Jesus was the bearer of their Christ, that in his life the God-for-us act and presence had uniquely occurred, they proclaimed the Christ as an event within a person (they spoke of "Jesus Christ" or "Jesus the Christ") and knew it to be an event that had changed their perception of what it means to *be* and of what it means to taste a full and conscious relatedness to that Center of irreducible Being in which all existence and all relationship lie. In conventional theological language, the Christ became for them the Self-disclosure of God and the presentation of his grace, winning them back from estrangement and self-centeredness to joyous relationship with their Creator.

God impinges upon us. "In him we live and move, in him we exist." This luminous sentence from Acts 17:28 (NEB) implies that God is more fundamentally related to us than our own thoughts, yet thought, always tied to images and symbols of finitude, can never capture the character of God, for neither we nor our thought are ever coextensive with God. God is our power to be, yet he is also the power to be of all *difference*, so that

THINKING ABOUT THE UNTHINKABLE 39

difference is no less real than am I. Thus the Christian must say that all particularity is real and as unique as it seems, that God is infinite and therefore immanent in all existence, and that individuality, otherness, even alienation, are as firmly grounded in the reality that is God as are identity and sameness. That there is no available logic which would permit him to say all these things without some incoherence is a fact that the Christian must accept until he learns a logic of infinitude.

At times Christians find it necessary to stress the otherness that separates us from God and from one another; this occurs usually in romantic eras such as the present, when prevailing fashions of thought tend to obscure or deny otherness and to absorb every thing into some unitary All. At other times Christians must stress the unity of God as the power to be of all that exists, because prevailing thought at such times is emphasizing separateness and individualism. But in any complete picture of his thought the Christian must affirm both the unity of God and therefore of Being, and the reality of particularity; that is to say, he must assert the being of otherness and of oneness, of difference and sameness, and he must not be trapped into denying either of these poles of our experience. As we shall see, it is precisely because Jesus is recognized as the Christ that we are bound to affirm equally the One and the many, Eternity and time, Being and particularity. But the problem of stating these essentials unambiguously compounds the already insurmountable difficulty of thinking or expressing God.

But while thought can never fully comprehend and describe the unique wholeness of God, it remains necessary for us to think, since to fail to do so would be to abdicate a role and a responsibility that God himself has presented to us in our evolution as thinking animals. We *must* think, but we cannot think God. That is our problem.

It is also true that in an important sense I cannot think any other person. I cannot, as it were, realize, appropriate in my mind, and in effect become identical with the full reality of my wife, my children, my friends. I can and, happily, do meet the gentle resistance of their integrity, and this meeting is the richest, although the most disturbing, kind of experience. But the persons-in-themselves remain other than I. If I think I have fully grasped and comprehended one of them, I have in fact merely closed myself to him, lost him, filled his place in my awareness with myself in order to obliterate the sometimes uncomfortable and always elusive integrity of his real otherness.

So I can no more think or speak the centeredness of another person than I can of God. Yet I cannot doubt that when I look into the eyes of someone a genuine mutuality may begin, a real meeting, and when I speak of him I speak of this betweenness, of something that has caught him and myself and been a sort of link. I did not become him; he did not become me; yet I can say something about him that is more or less true because it is what he truly contributed to that new entity, the relationship between us. So I say "John is a very kind man." And I mean that the relationship between John and myself or between John and someone else was enriched by his contribution of kindness. Whenever I speak about my friends, about their qualities and characteristics, I really am speaking about this "between-us" which runs into our separate realities so that there is no way of marking where each of us ends and it begins. And as God is the inclusive Being in which I am, so is he the Being within which relationship is.

Perhaps it is worth noting, as no more than an aside, that since relationship does not begin where I end, but issues from me and from the other simultaneously and most wonderfully, it is pointless to indulge in old philosophical games in which one tries to show the incoherence of pluralism or of a relational philosophy by arguing that these lead to an infinite regress, another relation being needed to relate me to the first relation, a third to relate me to it, and so on *ad infinitum.*

Relationship as the emerged continuity with distinction between another and myself is the occasion and the real substance of all our conversation about each other, and Christian theology is the discussion of a relationship so vast and deep that it gathers into itself all our other relations, which come to be seen as aspects of it. Of this we must say more later, but let us now establish one point: theology is about relationship, and theological language must, therefore, be appropriate relational language. We can begin, however, to suspect the difficulty of devising such a language if we consider the problem men have had in finding a satisfactory model of the relationship they wish to affirm between God and the universe, so perhaps we should spend a little time with this.

Eliot Deutsch remarks, "Logically, as pointed out by many a philosopher, one simply cannot have the full reality of a transcendent God and the full reality of the world."[3] This contention is actually quite inaccurate as it stands, for there is no problem whatever in having a real, transcendent God and a real universe if we grant that both are finite. This is the belief in all polytheistic systems, where the gods are found to be limited not only by the universe but by each other. The problem to which Deutsch points is that it is hard to account for a real, transcendent, *infinite* divine Being who is different from—that is, quite other than—an equally real universe. That this God is infinite, without limits, means that nothing *can* exist that is other than himself.

Now, Christians have held to the infinite being of God and have sometimes called him by such names as "Being-itself," so either they must agree that the universe is not other than God (its apparent otherness being less than real) or, if they want to maintain that the universe does indeed have some sort of reality as God's creation, they must find a way to symbolize the status of that universe in relation to the infinite God. Here is the fundamental question: in what way can God and the universe both be conceived or spoken of as real if God is infinite? Or, how is the infinite God related to the universe of our daily experience?

There have been a variety of models for discussing this alleged relationship, and I shall borrow some used by Robert C. Whittemore a few years ago in an article about Jonathan Edwards.[4]

If we use circles to symbolize God and the Universe, some of the most common ways of discussing the relation of the two are as follows:

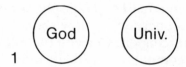

1

Here, God and the universe are considered quite separate and must, consequently, both be thought of as finite. Despite this limitation both are quite real, but the question of the relevance of God is urgent: since God and the universe are transcendent of each other they may actually have no relationship at all.

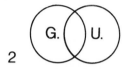

2

Here, God intersects with the universe: there is something of each within the other. It is sometimes said, in this context, that the universe is real to the extent that it participates in God and unreal or illusory otherwise.

3

Our third model represents classical pantheism. God and the universe are identical. The universe, seen truly, is God: God, seen inadequately, is the universe. It is sometimes explained that the universe is real *as God*, but as universe it is only appearance.

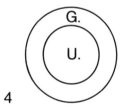

4

This is panentheism ("all within God"). The universe somehow exists within the being of God but does not exhaust God's being. The universe is finite but exists within the infinite God.

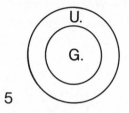

5

In this diagram God is represented as finite and as having his existence within the universe. He may be the God of a particular region or society, but in any case he is less than the universe.

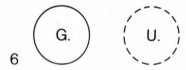

6

Christian Neoplatonism is depicted here. The universe exists as a kind of image of God: it is real as an image or shadow or projection, but it is no more real than a reflection or an idea is.

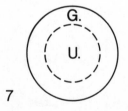

7

This model resembles panentheism, except that the universe contained within God is here thought of as unreal, except perhaps as an idea of God or something of the sort.

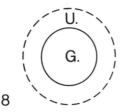

8

Finally we depict here the situation of a real God who is contained within an unreal universe. This can hardly be considered a widely popular option, but occasional suggestions of such an idea have been made.

The Christian is not committed inescapably to any of these images or theories. He wants to find a way to express God's relation to the world, and he requires that this expression shall be consonant with the experience of God-in-Christ, which is the Central Generating Experience of his faith; this leaves him with quite a high degree of flexibility. But he must speak about that relationship, and he must therefore choose a model for it which will do less injustice than other models to the reality of his experience.

The Christian's experience tells him (1) that material existence is important and not to be dismissed as mere illusion (because God acts within it in the Christ); (2) that *particularity* is also valuable and to be taken seriously (since the Christ is a unique, particular event in a unique, particular person); (3) that the presence of God (called, in conventional theological language, the Holy Spirit) is always everywhere; and (4) that material existence is of sufficient value to invoke God's saving activity, yet is inadequate to define God (since to be material is to be limited as God is not). From these observations it follows that we can accept no model for

speaking about God and the world that utterly separates them, makes either unreal, makes God less than
the universe, or simply identifies God and the universe.

Historically, Christians have made much use of our
sixth model, but to many moderns this seems to sacrifice too much the seriousness of human alienation
from God by making it, perhaps, merely the "image"
of rebellion. Nevertheless it is a useful and enduring
model. More commonly in recent Protestant thought
the fourth of our models, panentheism, has served
theology's purpose. This model enables one to suggest
that God and the universe are both real, although the
latter has its reality within the reality of God and thus
does not limit him by external and total otherness. Yet
the universe has some kind of authentic otherness
within God. Of course, we must remember that to
speak of "external" and "internal" here is merely to
find suggestive words, not to affirm that the world is
literally a sort of parasite disturbing the digestive or-
gans of deity. Relation between the world and God,
then, is always present but may not always be explicit
to the awareness of the world's individuals. No one is
without God, but many are without awareness of God.
Resistance and rebellion are real enough, but these can
have their existence only within the reality of God:
rebellion cannot *be* without absolute dependence on
that against which it seems to be directed!

Without doubt there are problems for reason in this
fertile image, but it enables us to say a great deal that
Christians find supported in their experience. As we try
to speak from within its general frame of reference,
however, we shall still find our words stumbling. It may
be useful to think of myself as existing within the reality
of God, but it is *I* who exist thus and I must still explain,

if I can, how that "I" and that embracing God relate to each other.

There is our difficulty. For the truth is that we have never discovered an adequate language of relationship; and our theology tends, therefore, to separate what should be together and to betray a bias of isolated, self-conscious individuality. Why this is so and what we may do about it (that is, how we may begin to think the relation with God and to express relationship at all) is the subject of our next two chapters. In concluding this chapter, let us add a note about our use of certain kinds of words.

When we say that for Christians the universe is "real" and exists within the being of God, we utter words that certainly present difficulties and are almost unintelligible if understood on the basis of some rather common presuppositions. It must therefore be said that to use such expressions theologically is by no means to use them in an ordinary, everyday, literal sense. Rather, we use words like "real" in theology in an almost negative way—to indicate what may *not* be affirmed. So if we say that the universe is "real," we mean that it cannot be treated as "unreal" and cannot be thought to be an illusion that authentically vanishes when truth is understood. As a "real" lake stands to a mirage, so the "real" universe stands to a philosophically "ideal" one.

Again, when we say that God is "infinite" and "immaterial" we are not describing him, but restricting what can be said about him. That he is infinite, for example, does not refer to his *size*, for God cannot be thought of in such terms without gross error. It means that he cannot be wholly "other" than anything that can truly be said to exist, for he cannot be bounded or limited in any sense by that which exists beyond him.

And to say that he is immaterial is, in effect, to indicate that, whereas things in general can be found at any one time in only one place ("I can't be in two places at once!" as mothers frequently complain), God is beyond the categories and limitations of spatial extension or temporal location. In simple terms, God can be everywhere at once because he does not have the qualities of matter, which would confine him.

Thus a "real," finite universe is limited in ways that an equally "real" but infinite God is not: yet it has a status, we must emphasize, quite other than illusion or mirage. Its reality is one with the reality of God, upon whom it is dependent; but because it is his act and not merely his thought, it is not in danger of vanishing if he ceases to "think" it, and it cannot be abolished by human efforts to rise above it in thought or in some mystical intensity.

A "real" universe is one with which we have to deal seriously; but a "real" and infinite God is the breath of our breathing and the life by which we live.

PART TWO

THE
LANGUAGE
OF
THEOLOGY

CHAPTER 4

The
Language
of
Relationship

"Doesn't the idea of a great, inclusive Oneness in which all differences are lost forever thrill you?"

"I'm afraid not. In fact, the remote possibility that it might be true depresses me."

"Why?"

"Well, there's a certain faddish favor for monism now, but there are kinds of dualism for which a great deal may be said. I'd rather sleep with my wife than masturbate, for instance. But, more seriously, I'd rather sit quite silently with any of my dearest friends than sit alone."

"But that's only because you feel insufficient; you don't like being alone, because when you are, you feel weak and small and temporary. And don't forget that the 'One' I'm talking about brings you and your friends together in the most marvelous way. All the barriers are down."

"Maybe, but I'm not sure that the experience of need being met is not after all more delightful than the experience of having no need. And as for the 'barriers down' business, that's the part I really don't fancy. You think the breaking of those barriers would enrich me, and in a way it would; but it's an enrichment I don't want to pay for. Don't you see that it's precisely the otherness, the sweet resistance of my friends that would be gone? But it is just that resistance that I find so unspeakably real and precious. You and your friends, who talk so much about the loss of your ego in the great Cosmic Mind, seem to me to be the greatest wanters in the world. You want so much that you won't be satisfied until the universe is yours—and yours in the tightest way imaginable. You want to BE the universe.

Now, I want much less. I want to be an atom in an infinite richness. I want love to be possible, not as a state eventually to be transcended in oneness, but as the flavor of my being. And that requires —yes, REQUIRES—an otherness which I cannot violate or own, but which must open to me like a flower, not to be robbed or plucked, but simply . . . loved."

We have said that Christian theology can dismiss neither the all-inclusiveness of God's Being nor the reality of the otherness between persons and between God and mankind. But our language, and even our thought, has difficulty when we try to do justice to both these aspects of truth.

The search for an adequate language is endless, and every generation coins its new forms of expression and tries to find better ways of viewing things. In the deadly serious enterprise called philosophy much time is spent honing impeccable sentences which, to the extent that they manage to avoid everyone's warnings and criticisms, usually cease to communicate anything of value for life.

A major problem in our language is that it arises from a questionable perception of the real character of our life. Monists, who want strenuously to affirm the oneness of all that is, often lament that they have no suitable terminology in which to do so, because all our systems of logic and syntax are based on dualism—the experience of a separation of reality into subject and object, self and other, and so on. Obviously a proper sentence does indeed consist of a duality: subject and predicate. This means that if the unlucky monist tries to tell us that he has experienced intuitively (or any other way) the unity of all things, he has already been betrayed by his own words. In speaking of his unifying experience, he has had to divide it into an experiencer, an experience of unity, and a multiplicity of things that have been experienced as one.

Of course, the monist has an even more serious dilemma. If he tries to persuade me that his view is correct, he is evidently demonstrating its inadequacy by that very act. His effort to teach me anything is a dualistic enterprise seeming to offer evidence that, whatever his theory, in practice he believes that I am as real as he and that my illusion or ignorance really exists to be overcome, just as his wisdom exists in opposition to it. So the monist's language and every *act* deny his protestations of cosmic oneness, for in an authentic oneness there can be no action.

It is less frequently noted that *relationship* between persons also has no suitable language. This is because our languages are not simply dualistic in form, but are also objectivist. By this is meant that they arise out of the experience of individuals who see everything as "out there," little solitary centers of awareness who seem spontaneously to treat all otherness as if it were *wholly* other. We speak as if we were each an encapsulated drop of "self" surrounded by similarly encapsulated, hermetically sealed objects. And when we want to speak of relationship between us, our language even encapsulates the relationship and speaks as if it were another object, a third thing alongside us.

To most of us, our usual subject-centered, objectivizing way of thinking and speaking appears to be more or less inevitable. A dramatic moment in Western philosophy arrived on the day when René Descartes (to whom subsequent speculation owes an incalculable debt) decided to try to find an indestructible basis for human understanding by calmly and systematically questioning everything he thought he knew in order to see if there was anything beyond the reach of doubt. He discovered that most of the axioms of his thought were quite easily doubted, and it must have seemed that a serious erosion of confidence in any knowledge was about to begin.

At last, however, his accelerating doubt reached a block. I like to think it was with a sudden jolt of delighted recognition that he saw in his mind an image of himself sitting there, busily doubting, and then knew that the one thing he could not possibly doubt was . . . that he was doubting!

One of my favorite images from the history of philosophy is that of Archimedes immersed in his bath, finding himself lighter (by an amount equal to the weight of the water displaced), supporting himself by one finger, and ecstatically screaming "Eureka!" Another is that of Descartes emerging from his introspective huddle and shouting the catchiest phrase to occur in philosophy for centuries: *"Cogito, ergo sum!"* meaning "I think, therefore I am!" Here was a rock that would not roll, and on it one might build a mountain of metaphysics. Who could possibly question a foundation as self-evident as this?

As a matter of fact, Descartes's exuberant formula is quite easily doubted, as subsequent philosophers recognized. His subjective experience of doubt really gave him no grounds whatever to be sure that anything existed except the doubt itself. His certainty that there was an "I" that was *doing* the doubting or thinking was an inference unsupported by reliable data. "I doubt, therefore doubt is" would have been a safer formula.

The important thing for us to see, however, is that Descartes went on to think of his "self" in a way that has characterized Western metaphysics ever since. He wrote:

I do not now admit anything which is not necessarily true: to speak accurately I am not more than a thing which thinks. . . . I am, however, a real thing and really exist; but what thing? I have answered: a thing which thinks.[5]

It will not be necessary for us to pursue in detail all the ramifications of this idea, but one of them is very important indeed. Descartes has really made thought the essence or character of selfhood; and he has thereby effectively separated the self from all other things, including other selves. *The self may be said to be a subject that knows or experiences ideas.* We may choose to think that some of these ideas are produced by actual sensory perceptions; that there really *is* an apple when we seem to see, smell, feel, and taste one. But this is strictly an assumption, since these apparent sense impressions may exist only as ideas and may not really be modes of contact with any "outside" reality at all.

We are saying that if one begins with the idea of the self as a thinker or experiencer of subjective impressions, in short, as a subject, one inevitably has a problem to account for any confidence in the reality of other objects. The self that is pure subject is locked up in its own subjectivity and can only *suppose* that there may be a world "out there" that more or less corresponds to the images of it which the self's thought entertains. Plagued by anxiety and frustration, the subjective self may even, one desperate day, decide to stop affirming the reality of anything else and be satisfied to believe that pure subjectivity is all there is. Such a drastic step removes all enemies and dangers except starvation, but the consequent tranquillity does not prove it to be correct, and to escape starvation one must pretend that food is real after all, or that the illusion of eating is a curiously important one that must continue to be fostered.

Western philosophy since Descartes has struggled with the task of accounting for, or denying, our confidence that we live in a real world and have authentic knowledge of it. But neither the affirmation of the world nor its denial can be perfectly persuasive: could this be because our philosophy, in beginning with the self as subject, has begun in the wrong place?

A continuing problem, then, for those who would speak about reality, is to find a way of thinking and speaking which overcomes the formal separation of subject and object that arises sooner or later whenever we begin with the conviction that the basic reality of our experience is *cogito*, i.e., thought or subjectivity. Suppose for a moment that subjectivity is *not* the first great fact of life; suppose it is even a faulty image upon which to interpret our experience of subjectivity itself! This is not to deny that we think or know, it is not to claim that we are not subjects who experience things, but it is to raise a question about the very ground, the premise or presupposition on which we understand our own acts of understanding.

Is there an alternative? Is there another place on which to stand in order to view more accurately the realities of life? I believe there is, and that it has been suggested by the British philosopher John Macmurray in his works *The Self as Agent* and *Persons in Relation*. The remainder of this chapter will attempt an interpretation of certain parts of Macmurray's position in the hope that we shall then find ourselves with a better than purely subjectivist point of departure for philosophy and theology, and with a linguistic tool that will serve to explore some of the most important ideas about God and man.

The Self as Agent

Macmurray's objective is to find what may be called a "logic of relationship," since he is convinced that relationship and not singularity is the main victim of our linguistic inadequacies. At the outset he rejects as a starting point for thought or for logic the Cartesian subject-object dualism, since, as we have seen, this makes the reality—to say nothing of the expressing—of relationship dubious at best. He illustrates the chronic failure of subject-object language structures to do justice to relations by reference to several adventurers in Western metaphysics, notably Hegel, who resorted to a kind of idealistic absolutism in which the authenticity of particulars is prejudiced; Kierkegaard, who wanted to defend existential particularity but became mired in radical subjectivity; positivists, who retire into semantics and seem to lose sight of our problem altogether; and existentialists, who, failing to find a logical form that will bear their message in formal philosophical adequacy, tend to write more effectively in drama and the novel.

Macmurray points to the dominance in the West of linguistic and existentialist philosophers as an indication of the impasse to which our problem of personal expression has brought us. Language philosophers tend to see our philosophical dilemma as a crisis of logical form, and existentialists see it as a crisis of personal life and expression. Macmurray feels that both are correct —as far as they go. The real problem to which we must urgently address ourselves is that of finding or constructing "the intellectual form of the personal."[6]

Another way of seeing the problem is through William James's familiar distinction between the "concept" and the "percept." A concept is an idea, a formal thought structure that can be applied again and again when it is felt to be relevant. For instance, the word "human" expresses an idea that is very useful when we want to specify a certain type of entity over against others (the "not-human"). Concepts, then, are abstractions and intellectual conventions that conveniently name or specify things. Percepts, on the other hand, are not abstractions or intellectualizations at all but are direct experiences, immediate perceptions or intuitions. If I were suddenly to confront a Martian one evening, my unreflective, immediate experience of him (it?) would be a percept; when, half an hour later, I tried to name and explain what I had seen I would be trying to form a concept. Percepts are private, and we can only communicate about them as we abstract from their concrete immediacy an idea or concept.

Now, language philosophers have tended to argue that concepts are the business of philosophy, that the task is to examine critically and precisely the way concepts are used, the variant character of concepts—in short, the "language games" in which meanings are conveyed. Existentialists, however, have expressed disenchantment with this preoccupation with concepts—mere intellectualizations—and have wanted philosophy to find a way of expressing percepts, direct, fully personal immediacy. Existentialists want to deal with life. Linguists want to deal with words about life. Here, then, is the impasse in modern Western philosophy. If concepts are only intellectualizations, they surely do not reach the beat of life itself but are mere driftwood on its surface; but if percepts are private, immediate, and subjective, they surely *cannot* be communicated and perhaps we had better leave them alone.

Is there, then, a way to bring together in speech my inner, subjective, and immediate experience and that other or outer reality which is not reducible to my subjectivity, but which—when I engage with it—calls into being concepts (as tools of communication) and seems to be the awakener of my subjectivity itself?

Immanuel Kant had wrestled with this problem and, although John Macmurray finds the usual difficulties in Kant's conclusions, there is one of them which might have served as a fresh point of departure. Kant has concluded that *reason is primarily practical.* This is the terminus of his thought, but it ought to have been the point of a new beginning, for it takes us suddenly beyond the premise with which Kant has labored throughout his work: that reason is primarily theoretical and the *cogito* a proper image of the human self.

Following this suggestion by Kant, Macmurray's aim is to abandon Descartes's starting point (subjectivity) and begin, as existentialism tries to do, with the fact of existence and to assert that "to exist is to have a being which is independent of thought." He reasons that "what depends on thought for its being is no *thing* but a mere *idea.*" [7]

In other words, when I become aware of you my percept is not sufficiently explained by reference to something going on inside my head; if it were, I would be quite free to "do my own thing" whether this included loving you or killing you, because you would be as internal to me as the percept itself, and nothing that I did to you would have any significance beyond its significance *for me.* Macmurray is trying to argue that percepts are the creation of a relationship, not merely of the subjectivity of a solitary person. If he is right, concepts become important as ways of extending the relationship out of which the percept has arisen. We are not here arguing that all concepts are derived from sensory perception, be it noted; that is a different issue. But, insofar as percepts are the inward expression of encounter between a subject and an object, a concept may arise that is the *outward* expression or the rational formalization of the percept. When it does, the concept ministers to a continuing encounter.

Concepts, then, may contain within them and be formed by percepts; but the concept so formed and shaped functions to perpetuate and perfect (or, alternatively, to demolish, but in any case to deal with) the relation that gave birth to the percept. To argue, as some philosophers and many unphilosophical romantics have, that percepts are the stuff of life and concepts mere rational cages and prisons, is to miss the point. Percepts and concepts cannot be understood in their personal significance except as relating to each other.

In place of various idealisms of East or West, then, Macmurray is offering a "realism." Not content merely to affirm "things" as well as ideas, he will try to frame a logical form that will rescue things from their linguistic castration at the hands of idealistic, subject-centered modes of thought.

For Macmurray, then, to exist means not only to be independent of thought (so that an obscure mountain flower exists whether any thought contains it or not), but it means "to be part of the world, in systematic causal relation with other parts of the world."[8]

Now we are ready for Macmurray's declaration of the proper perspective upon reality and the adequate basis for a language of real relation: in place of Descartes's "I think" *(cogito)*, Macmurray begins with the experience, concept, and phrase "I do." And in place of the isolated subject, thinking in splendid loneliness, he has a subject in relation with others, not "I" but "you-and-I."

In short (but, alas, not very short!) the self is not now conceived as primarily subject at all, but as primarily agent or doer. Conscious life begins not with some untriggered reflection, but with encounter with that which is not myself, with impingement of the self and another, with action; and our philosophy and its language must do likewise. If it begins with thinking, everything will finally struggle to escape reduction to mere idea, and even defiant realism will tremble on the brink of an idealism that has the linguistic dice loaded from the outset.

So it is not self which stands at the foundation of our life and thought, but self-and-other. To see all that is meant by this we must now turn to Macmurray's view of the nature of perception, for this will clarify what it means to be an agent.

Perception of the Other

Among the various modes of perception there has been a traditional tendency for people to think of *vision* as the principal one and a paradigm for understanding all of them. This is very curious because vision is probably that sense which men can most easily live without, although none of us wishes, of course, to be deprived of it. Many people live lives of great fulfillment although blind, and there is some evidence that even acute deafness is more limiting. Certainly it is hard to imagine oneself with no awareness of flavor or scent, and to be without a sense of touch would surely mean not to be able to survive at all. Yet it is vision that captures our imagination.

This preoccupation with vision is unfortunate, for

seeing is not a form of perception that brings us into direct contact with an object. Rather, vision establishes a distance between subject and object, since if the eye is too close to its target, it cannot see it at all.

Macmurray protests this primacy of seeing and takes, instead, tactual perception to be primary. This is, of course, important for his doctrine of the self as agent, because "tactual perception is *necessarily* perception in action. To touch anything is to exert pressure upon it, however slight, and therefore, however slightly, to modify it. Visual perception, on the contrary, excludes any operation upon its object, and is a perception in passivity."[9]

Further, tactual perception is the experience of a resistance to my pressure, and in this experience I directly encounter the other. It is thus that a baby probably first becomes aware of both the self and the not-self, and Macmurray observes: "The Self does not first know itself and determine an objective; and then discover the other in carrying out its intention. The distinction of Self and Other is the awareness of both."[10]

The importance of the evidently simple point we are making is enormous. We are suggesting that there would be no experience of either self or other if both together were not the truth of our reality. The self in isolation or an object in isolation would be a mere abstraction from the perspective of our experience. We shall see in a moment that a consideration of the experience of infancy seems to support Macmurray here, but it is essential that we note clearly that the self-in-touch-with-another is here affirmed as the first and most important datum of experience, *not* the self as isolated thinker or experiencer. The self does not begin to experience until awakened by contact with that which is not itself, and thereafter throughout our life there is a hunger for such contact. One of the attacks launched centuries ago by Madhyamika Buddhists upon their more idealistic colleagues who insisted that the fundamental reality could be thought of as something like a cosmic Mind or Consciousness was the argument that Consciousness seems always to require an object to awaken it to action, and if the universe is thought of as simply a vast Mind and its operations, one wonders how the operations could ever begin.[11]

How tragic it is that, faced with the clamorous demand of children to touch, feel, taste, and smell, we deliberately try to restrict their experience to seeing! In a toy store every parent has known the exasperation of having his recalcitrant infant try to maul the things on display, and standard to our responses on such occasions is the cry, *"Look!* Don't *touch!"* Is it any wonder that thousands of persons grow up with a perverted fear of touching or being touched and, coincidentally, a hunger for touch that leads us at last to invent rather ridiculous therapies in which folk may learn the courage to feel each other? Sensitivity training, when it does not degenerate into insensitivity rituals, is little more than a groan arising in our collective throat because we have denied and curtailed the exercise of our primary sense—the tactual.

Perhaps we may even, as an injudicious aside, attempt here a dubious speculation about cultures. Could it be that a culture that uses the grasping and shaking of hands as the ritual of meeting is, whatever its failings, closer to recognizing the basis of personal reality than one that substitutes a non-tactual form of greeting? Of course one has known handshaking to be insincere, but does it not affirm, even then, the reality of the other and establish some sort of contact? Bowing may be in excellent taste—but it does rather leave the other to be merely a vision.

Macmurray has suggested, then, that tactual perception and not visual should become the paradigm for understanding all personal encounter. This confirms his emphasis on the self as agent, for to touch is a form of action and not merely of reflection. But if action is to be central to our concept of the self and, because of this, to the mode we shall adopt for expressing the personal, it is necessary that we clarify what is meant by this term.

Action

Action—"I do"—may, according to Macmurray, be analyzed and shown to possess two parts, "I move" and "I know." The meaning of movement is clear enough, but it is important to realize that by "knowing" he means an awareness of the self and other in relation, a kind of self-and-other-consciousness.

Movement and knowing are what Macmurray calls positive and negative poles of action, both necessary for authentic *action* to occur. If the "knowing" element were absent when we moved, the result would be not action but mere "happening" or "activity," and the latter are impersonal and nondeliberative in character. In other words, when we use the term "action" in the present context we do not mean a simple muscular reflex or an unconscious habit; we do not mean simple movement, but intentional acting. When awareness or knowledge exists within movement as a shaper of it we have *personal action;* when it is absent we have some other kind of motion.

To press our analysis further, each of the poles within action can itself be divided into a positive and negative aspect. The negative pole within movement is resistance, and if this were not present in every moment or instance of movement there would be a helpless collapse rather than movement. I could not even stand, let alone walk, without being a network of muscular resistances. The negative pole within knowing is ignoring; that is, selectively ignoring the vast mass of irrelevant facts. We must engage in this selective inattention to data during every moment of knowing, or we would be inundated with information beyond assimilation. We are always selective in our attention to the data available to sense or reflection, and it is the inattention or ignoring that makes coherent knowing possible.

We have disclosed, through all this, a pattern in the analysis of personal action: a positive pole which contains an essential negative within it. This pattern persists wherever we choose to examine personal reality. For instance, action always involves an election of one possibility and a consequent rejection of others, the election containing and being shaped by the rejections.

So personal action, as distinct from a mere impersonal event or nonintentional happening, *is a complex of positive elements, each of which contains and is constituted by its own negative pole. Here we have uncovered what Macmurray considers to be the essence of the personal, and the proper model for every proposition that tries to express personal reality.*

The importance of this understanding of "action" for our doctrine of the self as an agent should be clear: an action requires an agent and cannot occur without one. But the negative element of action is knowledge (which includes reflection), and it is in connection with this that the proper place of subjectivity is revealed. The agent-self is also a subject-self, subjectivity being the negative pole of agency. When I act my action includes, as formative within it, *intention* to impinge on something. When I reflect or think I give *attention* to a body of knowledge or opinion. The attention helps to shape and constitute my subsequent intention, so that once again we discover a positive element that contains its formative negative pole in the relation of subjectivity to personal agency.

There is another way of regarding *intention,* however, complementary to our first, a way that illuminates yet another facet of personal reality and its positive-negative character. Intention is intellectual; it is a conscious "plan." As such it requires, for effectiveness, that it be associated with motivation, this being something felt rather than thought. Of course, we sometimes act from motive without intention, but this is really the shape of *habit* rather than action; or we may sometimes have our intention drowned by an overwhelming motive (as in loss of temper), and we may intend to act in opposition to some felt motive, but we shall achieve this action only if our intention can summon as ally a sufficient motivating power. Thus, while intention is quite distinct from motivation, we find again a duality: intention (the positive) containing motivation (the negative) —and thus is seen the usual effective relation of rationality and emotion.

Our brief, and perhaps suggestive, but not exhaustive discussion of selfhood is now virtually completed. We have seen why no idea of "self" that is principally or entirely subjective will satisfy experience if we treat the latter with honest analysis. At the same time, we have disclosed a consistent positive-negative pattern, which we shall shortly present as the basis for a logic with which to discuss personal reality, and especially personal relation. Before going farther, however, let us detour briefly (in the interest of clarity and persuasion) to glance at Macmurray's suggestions concerning the development of a "self" during childhood, for here we shall find both a further illustration and an augmentation of the points already made.

Childhood and the Development of Self

A human baby is an extraordinarily insufficient organism. Unlike the offspring of many other animals, he is quite astonishingly ill-equipped to face the world into which he has been unwillingly cast. He is deficient in physical resources and in instinctual adaptation to his environment, so that if left alone for even a short time he would certainly perish. He is, as Macmurray aptly says, "made to be cared for."[12]

But there is one thing the human baby is well equipped to do: he can express his feelings of comfort or discomfort by means of sound and gesture. Indeed, it is from such expressions that we learn a significant thing. The child seems to express satisfaction not only for such organic needs as food but also for personal and relational experiences—cuddling—giving further evidence that he does not and cannot exist, physically or psychologically, as an isolated unit. He is born for relation. Obviously, the basic personal reality is not the individual alone, but the composite unit "you-and-I."

We have seen that a fully personal act includes the elements of intention and motivation, the first being intellectual and the second emotional. Now, a baby comes to us equipped with motivation in some measure and sort, but without the developed capacity for intention. It has often been suggested that the roots of motivation in the child are compounded of love and fear, and these remain the basic elements (the first positive, the second negative) of all subsequent human motivation. In the child, love consists of the sense of comfort that is communicated through his nonverbal expressions of satisfaction, and fear is germinally present as the discomfort felt in the fact of deprivation, including isolation. This bipolar motivation issues inevitably in overt behavior, and that behavior is essentially a form of communication. But communication is unsatisfying unless there is response, and therefore the primary and distinctive character of personal behavior is always a mutuality; if you fail to respond to my genuine self-communication, you thereby depersonalize me and we are to each other mere objects.

Thus, from the beginning the child is motivated to throw a bridge across the void between himself and others, and it is only as his efforts meet with response that he achieves the possibility of becoming authentically personal at all. Without a response of some sort from some kind of "other" he will, of course, die; but if the response were merely the meeting of physical needs for food and shelter, he would, even if remaining alive, fail to become fully personal, because the response he has met has not itself been personal.

A child begins his life with motivation already part of his equipment, but he lacks the more sophisticated and acquired capacity to *intend*. This means that he lacks the capacity for a fully personal act. In his first days of life, therefore, it is necessary that his motivation be joined and governed by an intention that is provided for him from outside, namely, from the mother (or that person, male or female, who is presently performing the mothering function). Soon the child begins to acquire knowledge in the form of a discrimination of that around him which is not himself but which is a resistance of some sort. The not-self is gradually itself differentiated, some parts of it being stolid resistance (the slats of a crib, for example) and others being responsive (the mother's act of feeding the child finally distinguishes her as other, since there is delay between the felt need for food and the provision of it, yet her responding makes her different from that which never responds).

With the birth of even this much knowledge a crucial corner has been turned in the development of the infant. Intention begins to loom as a possibility, bringing with it the capacity for personal action rather than purely emotive behavior and random gestures. This advance along the road to selfhood does not necessarily make life easier for the parents, of course, because there is now an intention operating that may often conflict with theirs, so that compromise or coercion become daily events.

But even with the ability to intend, the child is still enormously dependent. He will never become fully *in*-dependent, for John Donne's truth still holds, and "no man is an island." Indeed, if someone did manage to isolate himself from all others, he would face a struggle to avoid slipping into patterns of almost exclusively habitual and impersonal response to the world. But a child must move from the kind and degree of dependence experienced in infancy until he becomes an interdependent equal with other adults exercising a measure of autonomy (always relative) which does not alienate him from others but lifts his relationship with them to new heights of dignity and personal authenticity.

To summarize: having learned to say "you," the child simultaneously and by inference learns to say "I". The birth of self-consciousness is dependent upon the birth of other-consciousness, so that awareness begins in a sense of "you-and-I" rather than in a sense of isolated selfhood. This new awareness of self and other creates the possibility of intention, since the discrimination of the self makes it possible to think about the self and its needs. And this capacity to think, plan, and intend makes movement toward mature mutuality possible, thus displacing symbiotic dependence as the pattern of relation.

But how does a child develop a degree of autonomy or self-government? This is to ask how he develops as a personal *agent*, and the answer lies in a pattern of "withdrawal and return" that begins early and increasingly to characterize the relation of mother(s) and child.

The periodic acts of mothering (feeding, washing, clothing, and so on) set up a kind of pattern of withdrawal and return in the child's earliest moments. It is necessary that he learn to trust the faithful responsiveness of the mother with such confidence that he can wait, when necessary, for the satisfaction of a want. When she never fails to come, even though there has been some small delay between the baby's signal of distress and her arrival, there is gradually built up in the child a sort of basic "trust." Without the establishment of this trust, as Erik H. Erikson has ably pointed out, an important cornerstone in the infant's psychological development will be lacking.

So the consistent, reliable "return" of the mother is essential to the stability and confidence of the child. On the other hand, if this pattern of return were to continue unaltered, the child would probably continue as an utterly dependent infant—a phenomenon not unknown, indeed, in notorious instances of maternal overprotection.

It is necessary, therefore, that the mother's pattern of "return" when needed be interrupted at last. She must not only teach the child, eventually, how to clothe himself; she must oblige him to do so. She must reach the stage of encouraging—even requiring—him to feed himself, to wash himself, to do for himself an increasing number of the tasks she has formerly done for him. Now, this refusal to act for the child any longer in a particular want or need will probably be felt by him as a neglect, a failure of love, and as such it will evoke anxiety in the face of a felt isolation. Even the satisfaction of achievement when he finally accomplishes for himself the thing that has hitherto been done for him will not wholly mitigate this anxiety. "The child can only be rescued from his despair by the grace of the mother; by a revelation of her continued love and care."[13]

In other words, the mother must at last return again in a demonstration of love, seeking to make clear that this love itself was never really withdrawn.

Thus the relation of mother and child, when productive of health and maturity, is seen to be a pattern of withdrawal (the negative element) and return (the positive). There is danger in this pattern, for despair may flourish and never be overcome, but there is also the possibility of immeasurable benefit. The relation of mother and child may move from being one characterized by infantile dependence to one in which maturity and self-respect have made possible authentic mutuality between equals. And at this level the full richness of love becomes possible.

In actual experience it seems probable that the quality of love and wisdom that parents present to their children is never so nearly ideal that there is not some residue of covert suspicion or even hostility resulting from the withdrawals. Yet there is no other way for parents to lead their children toward maturity, and there is no necessity for the alienations wrought in withdrawal to be deep or hurtful enough to destroy love or ultimately to invalidate trust. If indeed "perfect love casts out fear," then the nearer to perfection our parental love comes, the more nearly will the wounds of withdrawal be healed.

Conclusion

From all that has been said in this chapter certain conclusions follow. First, *the self is constituted by its relation to the other.* As a person I begin to exist as one pole in the complex "you-and-I." This is demonstrated by a study of the development of personhood in infancy.

Secondly, *I exist primarily as agent.* This must be so because in pure subjectivity I am fundamentally separate from any "other" and withdrawn into myself; thus, I am no longer in the state of relationship that would establish me as a person. Of course it is possible, and possible *only*, in such subjective withdrawal to study or examine someone or something objectively. In the first stage of the state of withdrawal into subjectivity, I reduce all "others" to objectivity. In the final state of withdrawal, my subjectivity has so turned inward upon itself that all objects, including myself as objectively known, have disappeared from view. In the first such stage, then, it is possible for me to acquire a vast amount of accurate objective knowledge through detached observation. This is largely the mode of scientific investigation, and it has a very definite and appropriate place in the human enterprise. But detachment of this sort, withdrawal from active engagement and into the subjectivity of dispassionate observation and reflection, do not establish the kind of relation in which I came to be personal and must now nourish my authentic personal reality.

Thirdly, *the elements of personal being are found to be regularly of a peculiar structure: a positive aspect that contains and is even constituted by its own negative.* This we saw illustrated in the case of motivation (the positive aspect of which is love, the negative of which is fear) and also in the positive-negative polarities of intention-knowledge, intention-motive, withdrawal-return. Above all, this principle is illustrated by the structure of the self, which is found to be an agent who has within him as the negative aspect of his agenthood a subjectivity. The self is doer and thinker, agent and subject, but the thinking or subjectivity arises as a consequence of an initial encounter and exists thereafter formatively within and for the sake of action.

To summarize: the primary personal reality is "you-and-I," and within this reality both the "you" and the "I" are primarily agents and secondarily subjects, so that the basic personal or relational entity is a self that is agent/subject.

Here is a clue to the mode of expression that will be adequate to carry personal, relational truth. It must be a logical form that is able to express the proper juxtaposition of a positive and a negative. It cannot be a mathematical form of logic, for in mathematics a negative cancels a positive. Neither will dialectic suffice, for we are not dealing here with thesis and antithesis. Thesis and antithesis "represent successive phases in the development of a unitary system,"[14] as John Macmurray rightly remarks, and we seek instead a form in which we can represent the same self as being "at one and the same time both Agent and Subject."[15]

The logical form we seek, then, must be a proposition consisting of a positive that necessarily contains and is even constituted in its shape by its own negative. We shall devote the next chapter to an examination of this form, contrasting it with other logical patterns with which it is likely to be confused.

Later we shall find that our clue to personal logic is also the clue to an understanding of some central Christian doctrines.

CHAPTER 5

The Logic of the Personal

At the end of our last chapter we arrived at a description of the logical "form of the personal." It is necessary now to examine this a little more closely, and we may best do this by contrasting it with similar but significantly different concepts.

Dialectic

In the form of logic known as dialectic we are presented with two terms out of whose mutual harmony or tension comes a new, third term that is a more nearly complete expression of the truth than either of the original two. Probably the most familiar example of this form arises not directly from Hegel's dialectic but from Karl Marx's application of it to political history. We are confronted, according to Marx, with a conflict of social classes, chiefly today the middle class (or bourgeoisie) and the working class (or proletariat). These classes represent "thesis" and "antithesis," to use Hegel's terms, and their conflict must be resolved into some sort of synthesis. Marx held that, politically, this synthesis would be constituted by a "classless society." We may thus diagram the concept of dialectic very simply:

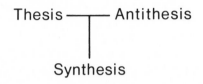

In a valuable article published in 1945, John Wright Buckham describes three kinds of dialectic: Decisional, Synthetic, and Evaluational.[16] Decisional dialectic may be characterized by Kierkegaard's uncompromising "Either/Or." Buckham says, "Having gotten both sides of the subject of enquiry, or situation, before the mind, fully and impartially," one then chooses between them.[17] This procedure is necessary when it is found that the thesis and antithesis with which we are dealing are mutually contradictory (i.e., one of the terms, if true, eliminates the other) or are in a state of contrariety (i.e., inherently hostile to each other). Contradiction is indicated in the sentence "My wife is partly pregnant," since the terms "partly" and "pregnant" are clearly irreconcilable and at least one of them must be rejected. Contrariety would arise if one wished to attribute goodness and evil to the same subject.

Synthetic dialectic moves more smoothly than decisional dialectic: it proceeds from the juxtaposition of the original thesis and antithesis to the production of a synthesis, more or less in the fashion Marx has indicated. But the synthesis that displaces the thesis and antithesis is never a merely mechanical joining of two terms or a fusion in which each original factor is utterly lost in a new neutral mixture. It is, ideally, something different from the original terms to whose existence both the original terms were necessary.

Evaluational dialectic is also synthetic in procedure, but it sees that one of the original terms is higher in value than the other and therefore gives priority to it in the formation of the final synthesis.

Buckham uses the word "contraplete" to refer to one or both of the original terms in a dialectic (i.e., the thesis and the antithesis). This is a useful and suggestive word, since it indicates that the terms stand in some sense over against *(contra)* each other, yet need each other for a statement of the complete truth. We shall continue to use the word "contraplete" to name the poles both of dialectic and of the "form of the personal," and we shall come shortly to examine the different ways in which these two systems approach their contrapletes. First, however, let us glance briefly at another form of expression.

Paradox

A paradox arises, contends Buckham, because of the innate polarity of truth. We find ourselves with concepts that seem to deny each other but that require each other in order to be understood. Here again we are dealing with contrapletes, and examples that come easily to mind are finite-infinite, divine-human, temporal-eternal.

It is a frequent and frustrating experience of some kinds of theology and philosophy to find themselves face to face with apparently irresolvable paradox in all directions. The bolder advocates of such systems often react by simply stating the paradox and leaving the stage, clearly suggesting that the paradox itself is the highest possible reach of human understanding. One suspects that many a sloppy mind has concealed many a feeble idea behind the facade of paradox, and has even earned applause as a guru for doing so!

At times, of course, a paradox may indeed be an inescapable verbal approximation of some truth, but very often it is nothing more than an arrested dialectic: it is the statement of the contrapletes without the next, the synthesizing or decisional, step being taken. In any event, paradox should never be accepted without struggle, for it offers a comfortable hiding place for ineptitude.

The Form of the Personal

The logical form that we are seeking to describe is neither paradox nor dialectic, but it *is* contrapletal. It is not paradox, because it does not bring us to an impasse in the expression of two apparently unresolvable yet mutually necessary terms. It is not dialectic, because it does not choose between its contrapletes, yet it also does not proceed through thesis and antithesis to a synthesis that gathers up the contrapletes into a distinctly new formulation.

Yet the logical form of the personal does recognize the duality of much truth, and especially the essential and unavoidable duality of personal or relational truth. It sees the human self as a duality of "I do" and "I think," and in the formation and growth of that self it sees the even more basic duality of "you-and-I." But it tries to find a logic more adequate than paradox or dialectic for the expression of personal reality, and it tries to derive that logic from the structure of personal reality itself.

Let us recall that Macmurray described the form of the personal as a positive that contained and was constituted by its own negative. If we were proceeding dialectically, we might place the positive and negative together and either decide between them or move through them to a synthesis. This is not Macmurray's procedure. The positive contraplete is the formal statement, but it must be shown to contain within it, in a constitutive way, its own negative. Thus, when we say "the self is agent" we are speaking the truth; but it can only be agent because it is also subject or thinker—otherwise its actions would not be intentional, which would mean they were not personal acts.

Now, it seems that the words "positive" and "negative" are likely to be misleading in our context. They suggest contrariety rather than completion, and for this reason I propose to substitute "formal" and "structural" for them, respectively, throughout the remainder of this book. The new terminology is not without its difficulties, but as we discuss further the role of the contrapletes in the form of personal logic, the reasons for our change will, I hope, become intelligible.

We have already used a simple diagram to illustrate dialectic; how may the form we are now discussing be imagined? Let us consider the relation of one contraplete to the other in the logical form of the personal. The formal (or positive) contraplete has to contain the structural (or negative) one, just as the agenthood of the self contains its subjecthood. This means that the structural aspect is related to the formal much as, for instance, metrical form is related to a whole poem. Let us take Byron's "The Destruction of Sennacherib" as an example of poetic structure and form:

The Assyrian came down like the wolf on the fold,
And his cohorts were gleaming in purple and gold . . .

If one reads this imaginatively, one finds that he has not only learned a few snippets of information or misinformation (about the dominant colors of Sennacherib's cohorts, for instance), and he has not only been told a story. He has actually *sensed* imaginatively the fearful excitement that men may have felt before the on- slaught of the Assyrians. Nor are the words alone re- sponsible for this effect. The even, measured meter of the poem suggests to the imagination the advance of cavalry. Even the least equestrian among us can see, as it were, the riders bouncing in their saddles when we say aloud, "The As*syr*ian came *down* like the *wolf* on the *fold.*" In a sense, then, the character of the final poem is determined by the meter that the poet has used. It contains and is constituted by that meter, and the meter may therefore be called, in a sense, the "structural" element of the poem.

No doubt one might select the relation of line or composition in a finished portrait as another illustration of what we are describing, but it may be most instruc- tive to flaunt elaborate imagination a little and think of an old-fashioned cart wheel—with a difference. Let us, then, imagine a wheel in which the two important ele- ments are a rim and a hub. This presents little difficulty, but let us further imagine that the rim actually derives its shape in significant measure from the hub, so that if the latter were to change its shape, becoming oval, irregular, or (incredibly) square, the rim would follow suit. From the perspective of the road, the rim is the truth being encountered, but that rim contains and is constituted in its present form by a hub. It can be distin- guished from the hub, yet it would cease to exist if the hub were not there.

This improbable wheel resembles the form of per- sonal logic. A personal proposition will be found to con- tain two contrapletes, which do not negate each other, and which do not need to be resolved into a new synthetic proposition, but which together constitute the truth. And one of these contrapletes will contain the other as its structural element.

As a demonstration of the potential of our logic, let us examine, by its light, two words that are often thought to be irreconcilable—words that dialectic attempts to deal with in its own way, but that are actually united in personal logic in the only way really according with human experience. They are the intensely relational words "love" and "hate."

If a dialectician were to become concerned about his being torn by conflicting love and hatred, he would possibly decide that his best course of action would be to work through these feelings to some sort of synthesis. The kind of synthesis he obtained would, of course, be determined by his predilection. One man might try to find a way of letting the love and hatred modify each other until they were replaced by a new feeling that was neither. Another man, operating on the basis of evaluational dialectic, might place a higher value on love and strive for a synthesis in which there was, indeed, mutual modification, but in which love was more determinative than hatred. A third man might operate in the area of decisional dialectic: he would recognize that love and hatred were incompatible and that he had to choose between them and strive to let the elected one drive out the other entirely.

None of these suggestions would be adequate for personal life. Love is important to us, and we would sacrifice much if we allowed it to be displaced by something which, as a synthetic product of love and hatred, were other and less than love. Yet it is unrealistic to think that hatred can, by force of will, be driven out. The fact which we all experience is that we *do* love and we *do* hate, and sometimes we both love and hate the same person or thing. It is not uncommon for us to love and hate ourselves.

Many persons, influenced by simple absolutisms and rigid moral standards, experience a feeling of guilt when they recognize their ambivalence toward a friend. They try to repress their hostility, as if it could be cut away and buried. But repressed hatred is not really destroyed, and it may work in us more insidiously than ever because we have begun to refuse to see it. It is the unalterable fact of our human ambivalence that makes any neatly logical analysis of our nature into separate aspects invalid, and it is our ambivalence that demands our attempt to formulate a logical form of personal reality which, in describing man, will not psychologically dismember him.

Men show both love and hatred. What is the relation of these apparently irreconcilable elements in our character?

First we must understand the bipolar nature of love. Erich Fromm has characterized love as containing care, respect, responsibility, and knowledge.[18] Accepting this as a reasonably accurate analysis of at least one kind of love, we discover that love as so described is really a contrapletal concept, because the percept on which our conceptualizing rests itself is complex. Each of the terms Fromm has used in his fourfold analysis belongs to one or the other of the contrapletes "love-as-active-concern-for-the-other" and "judgment," and of these it is the judgment which is the structural contraplete within love.

Love is a reaching out toward another for his sake. Therefore it does indeed entail care and respect and response-ability. But it is not a *blind* reaching out; if it is really to be love, it must contain knowledge and, with this knowledge, evaluation. Knowledge and evaluation together constitute what is meant here by judgment.

The importance of the contraplete "judgment" is seen when we consider what love might be without it. In point of fact, love is unimaginable without it, since love, lacking critical faculties, would resolve into either indifference or infatuation. For love to be real, it must see *the other as he is,* and it must promote a response to him by *me as what I am.* Mutual authenticity is quite indispensable here, but this means that he who loves neither wears a mask nor forces one upon his friend. To love is to accept perceptively even the faults of the other without either condemnation or approval, but it is never to pretend that our friend lacks the faults he has. "Judgment" is thus not blame or rejection, but honest awareness; and the "evaluation" within it is merely the frank recognition that, for better or worse, *my* values and style of life are different. Without judgment so understood, there can be no love, because either I refuse to take the other seriously or I refuse to be myself. It may be, of course, that what I see as a fault in my friend is not so at all: it may be a blazing virtue. But the point I am making is that until my values change, if it is seen as a fault when I look honestly upon him, I must not pretend that I see it otherwise. The mother who refuses to believe that her son could be in any sort of trouble does not really love *him:* she loves an ideal image which lives only in her mind and which she sees instead of him.

Now if love is of the nature we have described, it follows that the loved person—to whom we are "bound," but whom we know to be other than ourselves—constitutes a limit to our independence, and this will sometimes appear to us as a threat to our freedom. The greater the threat (perhaps because of the strength of our love), the higher will rise within us a fear that is our subjective reaction to threat. Macmurray has pointed out that love and fear are the basic elements in all motivation and that the dominance of fear, if it should occur, causes love to be displaced by hatred.

Since any love entails a limiting of the one who loves, it follows that hatred is always potentially or actually present. The presence of love and hatred together is not paradoxical, and the two are not to be resolved into a new synthesis. Rather, hatred is the symptom of a fear, perhaps not even acknowledged, and the road to health presumably lies in discovering the nature of this fear and allowing it its proper—but never an improper —place in our calculations.

An important question arises concerning the capacity of love (containing judgment) to overcome the various forms of unwanted separation between persons. It might seem that the element of judgment would ruinously reinforce the objectification of other selves in which we all indulge and by which we isolate ourselves in pride, anxiety, or lostness. To judge another is surely to remove ourselves from him, and a love that contained this must, it may seem, inevitably become mere patronage.

The truth is, however, that the kind of love we are discussing is precisely that which can precipitate the uniting of two persons while retaining the authenticity of each. This "uniting" is not a *merging* in which the individual integrity of one or both partners is sacrificed. In this uniting there is a mutuality of two centers of awareness and decision. The difficult task of maintaining this delicate balance of relatedness and integrity is possible for love, because love is itself a polarity of concern and judgment. If love were merely concern, the result might be the symbiotic absorption of the weaker by the stronger partner; if it were merely judgment, there would be simple separation. In its duality, however, love operates with a pattern of withdrawal and return that may assure the preservation of all that is best in the relationship itself and in the individuals concerned. For judgment does involve withdrawal into reflection and, to that extent, does indeed presuppose and maintain the identity of each love partner. But the withdrawal is for the sake of return and is contained within the larger context of the return, and thus it helps to make that return a meaningful encounter in which my response to my friend can be the more appropriate and responsible because of the reflection.

Two objections to our analysis of love seem likely to occur. The first is based on the Biblical observation that "perfect love casts out fear." If this is so, it might be argued, does not our whole discussion fall to pieces? Certainly not, for the contraplete of love is not fear but judgment, and we have only claimed that in human experience this, in turn, produces fear through the perceived threat to individual freedom. Only perfect beings could love perfectly; only a being unthreatened by anything "outside" or beyond himself could be free from the possibility of fear. We may therefore presume that God is able to love without fear and without hatred, and that the problem raised by the experienced antithesis of love and hatred would not arise if we were God.

The second objection is more likely to arise from the avid reader of "True Love" magazines than from Biblical students (although I would not want to claim that

these two classes are mutually exclusive). In the rosy
haze that surrounds the sort of love proclaimed by ro
mantic fiction, can there be any room for judgment? I
not the love that we are led to expect a sweet, uncriti
cal, exquisitely painful ecstasy? Are not all blemishe
swept aside by its puissant progress? Indeed they are
And many a credulous swain has consequently ex
perienced a marriage so thoroughly devoid of rea
knowledge and understanding that it was mere anima
mating, having little in common with authentically hu
man love.

To the extent, then, that the statement "I love you"
is true, it means also: "I *know* you. I really see *you*.
am aware that as an other to myself you are a resistance
I meet, a center of intention that will sometimes con
flict with mine. I know that you are not completely
altruistic, as I am not. In relating to you I am aware tha
you set limits to my possibilities even as, in other ways
you extend them, and I shall resent sometimes the lim
its and rejoice in the extensions. Because we are no
simply one person, there is both togetherness and
apartness for us. I approve of you in part and I disap
prove in part, but I care and want to respond to *you*
both approved and disapproved."

If, in fact, we do not mean all this when we avow love
we probably mean instead, "I intend to possess you so
that you will cease to be another person and become ar
extension of myself." Or perhaps we merely mean: "I
have a warm feeling about you. You are attractive, nice
company. But if you become inconvenient, I simply
don't care enough about you to get resentful. You are
expendable."

Thus it may be seen that "I love you," when spoken
truthfully, is a statement that contains implicitly its own

structural contraplete, "I judge you," and this makes it possible, indeed, humanly inevitable, that in part and at times "I shall hate you."

Conclusion

A statement that adequately conveys personal truth will be one that can be analyzed, and must be understood, as containing a contrapletal character, which is the verbal parallel of the polarities of personal life. One of these contrapletes we shall call the formal, for it is the one that most plainly and overtly presents itself for our attention. The other, the structural, lies within the formal, so that the latter is misunderstood if it is not seen to contain constituently the other.

We shall find that it is always important that the formal contraplete remain dominant, for if the roles are reversed, one is faced with a new concept (just as love turns into something else if its contraplete, judgment, becomes dominant).

Since theology is preeminently concerned with personal truths, it follows that, if Macmurray is correct, a theological statement must be expressed in terms that submit to the logical analysis we have proposed. It is to an examination of some ancient theological concepts that we next turn.

PART THREE

TOWARD
A
DIALOGICAL
THEOLOGY

CHAPTER 6

God:
A
Natural
Theology

"People who really know God don't try to talk about him. It's like that old Chinese saying: 'the Tao that can be named isn't the true Tao,' or something. Anyway, if you've really felt the great Mystery, you know that words are quite useless; they can't possibly reach it. Talking about God is like trying to catch a whale with a shrimp net."

"Well, that's true enough up to a point. But even to catch a whale you need SOMETHING. Do you mean to say that words have no use at all?"

"I just mean that God is the profoundest Mystery of the universe, and words are no use around it. Words are for working out meanings, and there's no meaning in Mystery. Mystery is just . . . mysterious! You EXPERIENCE it; you don't explain it or express it in words or meanings or reason of any sort."

"I don't entirely disagree with you; but I can't entirely agree, either. You see, there's a bit of a problem in this business of 'experiencing' God. I'm not denying that you can be sensitive to his presence within you or around you, but religious 'experience' is a bit like surfing: if you leap into the ocean, you know directly what it's like to feel the force of moving water, and you'll feel that any words about it are just not the same thing. No one's words are the same as the feel of cold, rushing sea. But if all you know is your own experience of the sea, you don't know much after all. You have no idea of the size of it, or its shape, or the curious things it may do in odd places. It's only when the experiences of a lot of people—and all the relevant experiences of those people—are put together that you can speak about the sea with any degree of adequacy.

With enough data you can put together a map that will tell you more than you could ever know by just surfing. That's why I want to talk about God, and to listen, too. My own thoughts about him, and even my 'experience' of him as a matter of fact, are always shaped by some ideas and prejudices I didn't even know I had, and it's good to speak and listen so that I can find my own secret assumptions and help you find yours. After all, if I only surfed at Waikiki I'd never know there are better beaches at Sydney!"

We have already said that God is unthinkable—beyond the reaches of the wildest (and especially the soberest) imagination. So he is beyond words, too. Yet we shall begin now to try to say something about him. Preposterous? Precisely! But we are verbal animals, and we must struggle to say something even about the farthest and most precarious reaches of our vision, or suffer like an egg-bound chicken. Of course, we must be careful not to let our words, shimmering insubstantially before us, become a substitute for that wordless Truth toward which they brokenly try to point.

There are two principal ways to approach a discussion about God. One such way is to limit ourselves to what our own reason and experience offer. Many people, unconsciously enmeshed in the "dogma of sufficient reason" are convinced that this is the only way we need. The other way, however, is to call upon some "revelation" to give us information or insight. We shall be contending that there is indeed a Christian revelation, and that it is unique and irreplaceable. But it may be useful to begin in what is usually called "natural theology" (that is, a theology that uses only resources natural to us all—reason and experience) and to begin with some ideas about God that are older even than Christianity. If we can see how "dialogic" helps to sort out an ancient problem or two, we shall be ready to let it explore the critical events and words of the Christian tradition. And we shall have laid a foundation upon which that tradition's "revelation" can build.

If we are to discuss God, we must first have at least a rough idea of what the word means, or we must agree about what it shall mean for our present purpose. Without doubt one of the most fruitful of recent suggestions is that of Paul Tillich, i.e., that "God" is, or should be, the term we apply to that entity which concerns us in an ultimate or supreme way. If a man's chief concern and loyalty is toward his nation (so that he would sacrifice everything else, even life itself, in the interest of his nation), then his nation is his God. If his highest regard is for his wife, children, money, power, or social position, then it is here that we find his God, or at least that which has the best chance of becoming his God. The question to be asked, then, is not whether a man believes in or worships God, but what God does he worship; it is not whether God exists, but what is the nature of God?

Clearly we are a polytheistic people, for among us many gods can be found. But is there one "true" God? Is there an entity or power or something that deserves —and alone deserves—our supreme loyalty, concern, and commitment?

Trying to remain within what clear reason can say without the aid of revelation, Tillich argues that the root of our existence, the very power in us to "be," must be of the greatest possible concern, for unless we *are*, unless we have "being," we can have no concern at all. It is, then, "Being-itself" that is truly deserving to be called, and regarded as, our God.

Whatever else we may eventually want to say about God, it seems reasonable to accept Tillich's suggestion as a starting point. If the name "God" is to be used at all, it is most deservingly given to him who (or to that which) exists by his own power and apart from whom nothing else is. The New Testament seems to nod approval by declaring that "in him we live and move, in him we exist" (Acts 17:28, NEB).

We may infer something about God, then, as we study our own being or existence. What is the form or character of our existence? That is to say, how do we experience life and, even more broadly, "being"—the facticity or "there-ness" of things?

Here we immediately run into some very honorable (because very ancient) philosophical puzzles. It does not take us long to discover that reality, as we know it, is torn between seemingly irreconcilable qualities or characteristics, so that the poor philosopher's effort to patch it up is like trying to make peace between a Titanic and its iceberg. Among these warring qualities we find permanence and change, and a question that has confronted men for at least three thousand years is whether one of these or the other chiefly characterizes reality at its deepest level. Is movement, change, process, flow, or whatever we want to call it the "real" nature of things? Is this, indeed, "reality"? Or is stability, endurance, stillness, sameness the "real"? To put our question in theological form, is God characterized by motion or rest; is he "Being" or "Becoming"?

This is an important question, for if God is thought of as unmoving, as stillness or rest, the world becomes quite inexplicable. How can it be? And if it somehow happens to be, how can we take it seriously? It cannot even be a good, thoroughgoing illusion, for the arising of an illusion, or even its persistence, is a process. Moreover, this particular "illusion" is one that includes all sorts of movement. So if we begin by thinking of God as "Being," we shall at last, perhaps, end by trying to ignore the world as if it were something the dog had embarrassingly deposited at a cocktail party. But if everything is just flux, we shall have trouble dealing with the persistences, the endurances in things. A table may be just a mass of atoms, but it is remarkable that in four hundred years someone will pay a fortune for it because it is still a table!

We are saying, then, that experience presents us with the impressions of both endurance and change. Is there a way of doing justice to both of them in our account of reality—and that means, in our account of God? Can God, the Ground and Anchor and Source and Power of all our existences, be somehow both movement and rest, being and becoming?

A similar problem arises with regard to another and closely related set of seeming irreconcilables: unity and plurality.

It is certainly true that mystics report an experience in which they feel that all distinctions have dissolved and everything has become One (or at least, as some of them would prefer to say, "not-two"). It is even true that we—including the least mystical among us—find within ourselves a longing for simplicity that may sometimes lead to a moment when the universe appears to us as a whole, an entirety—and that is why we persist in thinking of it as a *uni*verse rather than as a *multi*verse. Yet only obstinacy, surely, obliges us to ignore the fact that we also know our world as a set with many members; as the children's poem of Robert Louis Stevenson has it, "the world is so full of a number of things." So to see reality as *one* is to do an injustice to our experience; it is to refuse quite arbitrarily to take seriously some moments in it. Can reality (can God) be both one and many?

Western theology has had some bad moments. For a long time it was seduced by Greek philosophy, and one of the most unfortunate consequences was that it borrowed (stole, if you like) from the wrong Greeks a prejudice against motion, change, dynamic; consequently it developed an enormous appetite for the immobile, immutable, and quiescent. It spoke of God as an "Unmoved Mover" and made him eternally unchanging. Obviously this meant that anything that moves or changes was not God—and so Western theology found itself in a very precarious position indeed.

Happily, recent times have seen the slow growth of another and better sort of philosophy and theology. It too has roots in ancient Greece (especially in Heraclitus), but the contemporary version, stemming largely from the work of such men as Alfred North Whitehead, Charles Hartshorne, F. R. Tennant, Nicolas Berdyaev and Pierre Teilhard de Chardin (to name—somewhat arbitrarily—only a few) is often called "process" philosophy, and it is an attempt to do justice to the apparent polarities we have named. It tries to find ways of speaking about God (or about Perfection, or whatever name it gives to what is of ultimate value) in which, even within his nature, change is taken as seriously as permanence, unity as seriously as plurality. There are times, it is true, when process thought seems a little heavy-handed in its efforts to marry the polarities, as when Whitehead splits them between what he calls the "primordial" and the "consequent" natures of God: this is perilously like claiming to have reconciled bitter enemies so that they could live together under one roof, when one has, in effect, merely built an impenetrable wall through the middle of the house to keep them from troubling each other.

Despite such lapses, however, process philosophy or theology is certainly asking the right questions, and "dialogical theology" (or what we shall call "dialogic") should be seen as a species of it.

How, then, does dialogic help us to discuss our apparently schizophrenic reality? How does it account for such polarities as we have discussed, and how does it do so within the single character of God? To provide a pearl that we must next proceed to peel in order to appreciate, dialogic will deal with our polarities by understanding that they are not qualities in conflict at all; they are not separate and alien moments in God's experience. Rather, they are contrapletes and can each be most fully understood only when all are seen in their true mutual relations.

He Who Is

We are ready now to take our dialogic in our hands and to plunge, not indeed fearlessly but at least bravely, into a discussion of God. Is God Being or Becoming? Is he Unity or Plurality?

To begin with our first set of apparent irreconcilables: we can cheerfully say that since we are using the term "God" to refer to that which ought legitimately to concern us ultimately, he is inevitably the inclusive reality outside which nothing can exist. This, after all, must be the very ground and possibility of any concern whatever. Thus God is "Being," the "is-ness" of whatever is.

But God must also be Becoming, for we never experience Being—reality in us or around us—without sooner or later noticing that it has undergone change. Thus *God is really best thought about as Being/Becoming.*

Our opponent sharpens his knife. We have been found out in a subterfuge. We have reconciled our opposites by throwing a casual hyphen between them as if it were a drop of Elmer's Glue! But wait until we have pursued our thought a little farther.

What we are saying is that Becoming (movement, dynamic, process) is not an alien and uncouth intrusion into Being, but is the latter's very shape. Endurance *is*, but it is not lifeless and still. Reality is eternal persistence shaped by timely process.

If we recall our analogy, in an earlier chapter, of the poem about Sennacherib, we may say that Being is like the poem in its wholeness, its simple "being-there." But Becoming is the meter, the throb that gives it its distinctive flavor and kind of presence—its "being-there-like-that." Or, to revert to our formidable wheel, what meets us directly (the rim) is the sheer fact of a reality that always *is* (of a God who *is*, and whose character never suffers conflict yesterday, today, tomorrow); but it (or he) is *as it is* because the hub—its very character —is process or Becoming.

Just as it is the very nature of water to flow, so it is the nature of Being to become (to move, to undergo process). Yet as flowing is not precisely the water, Becoming is not precisely Being. Neither is itself without the other, and the reality we experience is the contrapletal relation of the two, and the two therefore are actually a whole, contrapletal *one*.

So God is Being/Becoming. Likewise you and I change, yet we are always you and I. And the worlds decay, yet worlds remain. All this is so because he in whom we live and move, who is our encompassing realy, is that permanence whose character is movement.

Alas, only the wearied professional theologian will
ccuse us so far of being clear. And that may be the least
f his objections. Can we attack our problem of discuss-
1g the character of God from another direction? We
re already so far into the absurdity of discussing the
ndiscussable that there is no reason to succumb to
1odesty now.

Let us make use of the other set of contrapletes to
·hich we have made reference: unity and plurality.
)ur question now becomes this: Are all the many
1ings of everyday experience really gathered into a
eality which—if only we could see it truly as the mystic
oes—is actually *one?* Or is that oneness an illusion, and
· reality irreducibly many? Is God best thought of as an
uncarved block" (to use a Taoist metaphor), a Unity?
)r is he a collection of things, a mass of particularities?
Ve are rather like a man who stands on a cliff and looks
own at a long, golden beach: should he think of it as
a beach" or as an uncountable number of grains of
and?

So: Is God one or many? Unity or Multiplicity? Uni-
·ersality or Particularity?

This is an important question, because if God—and
1erefore our very power to be—is *one,* we must ex-
lain (or explain away) our sense of personal and unique
1entity, our conviction that we are really different
·om our neighbor or our enemy, and our belief that if
· should happen to convert you to my point of view,
·omething will have *happened* that marks a difference
etween you as you were and you as you are and be-
·ween my mind and yours.

But if God is straightforward Particularity or Multi-
licity, we must accept the fact that mutual limitation

is the character of existence itself (i.e., that mutual limi
tation is just what is fundamentally real) and that there
is no encompassing relationship binding us together
and offering the hope of some inclusive meaning for all
our lives.

> One or many, which is He?
> If He's one, is that one me?
> Of course it is! And I insist
> Asparagus does not exist.

Our question, "One or many?" may perhaps be il
luminated if we imagine an improbable but not impos
sible scene. A man is sitting in mystical contemplation
having achieved a state of trance. He is oblivious to the
world outside and, in fact, he is experiencing "reality"
as an undifferentiated oneness. All distinctions are gone
from his consciousness and he sits there in the actual
experience of "not-two." All, for him, is a glorious and
eminent peace.

As our mystic sits there, a crude fellow with no mysti
cism in him at all (but a course in freshman philosophy
comes along and, recognizing a classmate whom he had
always bitterly resented, takes the opportunity to pick
up a stick and pound the entranced one on the head
Evoking no reaction (since for the mystic there is no
longer a distinction in consciousness between himself
his enemy, and his enemy's stick), the brutal intruder
strikes again and again.

Now, just what can be said to be "really" happening
here? If the mystic's state of mind reveals the truth
about reality, the hostile one is pretty hard to account
for as "real," since all is an undivided harmony—in fact
more than a harmony, a unity. But if the horrible assail
ant (probably a logical positivist) is correct, there is a

very real distinction between himself and the mystic, and the latter's trance state is merely a lapse into misleading subjectivity. On the other hand, if the attacker is quite correct in his sense of the radical otherness of his victim, can one really account for the exhilarating and mysterious interpenetration of our lives? For some of us it will not do to think of our deepest friendships as the mere bouncing together of two rubber balls: there has been an "at-oneness" that transcended our separateness. So maybe the mystic has something of the truth after all.

So we ask again: *is God*—the Reality outside whom no one can exist—*one, or a sort of plurality?*

It is time to resort again to dialogical structure and to argue that God is neither one nor many, but (if we must think about him) he can best be thought of as Unity/Plurality. God is one. But it is not his character to be a block. Movement is the shape of his Being, and movement requires distinction; this means that as Being is shaped by Becoming, its Unity is necessarily shaped by Particularity.

In other words: wherever there is motion, there is "here" and "there" (as the "places" from which and to which motion occurs), and there is "now" and "then." These are the modes of Particularity within time and space. Particularity, then, becomes the shape of Being (or Unity) as soon as we understand that it is dynamic and not static.

What we have said is still not embarrassingly lucid. Let us talk "around" our theme a little and see if a tortured gleam of light can break.

God can be known intuitively and directly in the experience of the mystic because he is Being, and because as such he embraces the being of the mystic himself. But mystical experience that annuls the sense of distinction or denigrates its importance must be illegitimate, because the Being of God (or the Being that God is) is not a solid, static, lifeless block (a sort of unmoving is-ness), but is structured by Particularity and the becoming (or process) of particular entities. If this were not so, we would have no world or even the illusion of a world, no problem for philosophy to solve or religion to overcome, for there would simply be the undifferentiated and eternally undeceived character of God.

In other words, if God (Reality) is simply *one*, there can never be a second, nor even the illusion of a second, for such an illusion would either be God (in which case there would be only the illusion) or would exist in addition to God (in which case Reality is not *one*). On the other hand, if God is simply multiplicity with no interpenetration of any sort, the experience of profound relationship and every movement in personal, social, and natural life toward convergence would be difficult to understand. So would endurance itself, for this is identity through a series of moments.

If, on the other hand, we think of God as Being/Becoming and consequently also as Unity/Particularity in contrapletal perfection, we have the ground for an acceptance of both change and endurance, of both distance and relationship.

God is Being. The worlds arise because it is of the very essence of God that Being find expression in Particularity. But he is always the Being of *every* Particular even as he transcends them all. *In him is the Being (the reality) of difference as well as of identity.* For this reason, the world's differences and particularities never vanish, even when our vision is most truly enthralled by the Unity of God.

God is Being and Particularity. Since Being embraces and is structured by Particularity, it follows that the flavor of Being must be a binding and envaluing of Particularity; that is to say, it must be a sort of love. Not, of course, love as a sentiment or emotion, not the cloying, destroying lust to acquire and enjoy that is romantic love, nor the consuming fire that often passes for parental love. The love that pervades Being as its way of embracing the Particulars that shape it must be an acceptance of each of them and thereby the investing of each with value. To our surprise, the Bible has anticipated us with the incomparably economical statement, "God is love" (I John 4:8).

We have now reached an interesting point in our discussion. All our speculation has brought us to the recognition that Being, or Reality (which we are calling "God"), is a Whole structured by Particularity, and that the flavor of that Whole must be a sort of love—that is, an envaluing of the Particulars within it.

But if this should be so, that necessary envaluing could hardly be complete without an act of some sort by which Being did indeed envalue the Particular; without the actual, concrete occurrence of such an act we are left with mere theory—just another philosophical premise. But if Being can be seen not only to be structured by Particularity but in some way concretely to *affirm* the Particular—ah, then we may have an occasion of awakening indeed and what we have said shall be no longer mere words but a way of describing an experience capable indeed of generating a religious tradition.

Has such a thing happened? Is there in our history an occasion when Eternity touched and affirmed the moment? Is there an event that envalues every Particular because it is the presence and act of the Universal within a Particular?

It is the astonished response of Christianity that the answer to these questions is a splendid Yes! As we examine the crucial occasion and event that is the focus of that Generating Experience of our Faith, we shall find ourselves confronted with the necessary and perfect expression of contrapletion, of personal logic personally expressed. And we shall learn to say a little more—still tentatively and still imperfectly—about God. We shall, in fact, have proceeded from natural theology to Christian theology.

CHAPTER 7

The Concrete Universal: Jesus the Christ

"I don't mind a certain amount of reverence for Jesus. Personally, I think it's healthy to have a set of saints to admire. Buddha, Abe Lincoln, Socrates, and Jesus: that's a pretty nice group to have as your heroes. But to talk about Jesus as if he were God is rank superstition."

"I agree. But to recognize in Jesus the presence of the Christ is neither to think of him as God nor as quite the same as Buddha, Socrates, or Lincoln."

"There you go again, worming your way around the problem. What I'm saying is that if Christians had been content to keep the TEACHING of Jesus—and especially the Sermon on the Mount—as their ideal, the church would have been much more effective. Instead, they get involved in a lot of hocus-pocus about what they call an 'incarnation.' Lots of religions have incarnations. Some old Greek gods were incarnated every spring, and Krishna was the incarnation of an Indian god who comes to earth any time he feels like it. The church should have stayed above all that nonsense and held itself responsible for passing on the clear, common-sense teaching of Jesus."

"I wonder whether you've ever really read the teaching attributed to Jesus—especially the Sermon on the Mount! It's pretty disquieting stuff—all about not looking lustfully at women, not relishing anger, caring for your enemy, and so on. But as for the incarnation' of the Christ, what we mean by that is really quite different from what your ancient religionists meant by it, and even different from the idea of Vishnu's avatars (such as Krishna). To 'see' what is meant by the Christ is like being hit in the face with a bucket of cold water—it's a real 'awakening.' It leads to seeing the world and everything in it in an entirely new light."

"Then you must be meaning something by the word 'Christ' that I didn't pick up in Sunday school. But then, apart from measles I didn't pick much up there anyway. What IS a Christ that a Buddha or a Lincoln or a Krishna isn't?"

In theology, "revelation" means that God is understood to have disclosed something about himself or to have presented *himself* to us. In Christian theology the supreme revelation or self-presentation of God is said to have occurred in the life, death, and resurrection of "the Christ," and a truly remarkable and even unique feature of this revelation is that it discloses the dialogical nature of Reality.

The Universal (God) appears to us in concrete particularity; the Eternal fills a series of moments: the "revelation" of the Christian tradition is therefore entirely at one with the demands of a dialogical view of things and supplies what that view requires if it is to be persuasive: the occurrence of the paradigm as concrete actuality.

Let us explore more slowly and, one hopes, more clearly the meaning of what has just been said.

We have seen, in an earlier chapter, that theology is one way in which people try to remember, explain, and precipitate anew the Central Generating Experience of their particular religious tradition. Now, the Generating Experience of Christianity is the awakening of the disciples and the first Christians to the "Christhood" of Jesus of Nazareth with all that this entails, and it is therefore the task of Christian theology, above all else, to explicate that Christhood and so to present it that a similar awakening may occur in other persons today. In approaching a discussion of Christ, therefore, we reach ıe heart of our project. We shall be trying to show how ialogic illuminates the meaning of Christhood in a re-·eshing way, but we should not proceed to that with-ut making some preliminary remarks about the gen-ral study of Christology, thus providing a context for ur present thinking within the broader scene of to-ay's theological enterprise.

One of the liveliest aspects of Biblical scholarship in ecent years has been the so-called "quest for the his-orical Jesus." This is, of course, an attempt to find in the New Testament at least fragments of a reliable "histori-al" record of the life and teaching of Jesus, fragments whose matter-of-fact accuracy may be beyond reason-ble doubt. No one denies that there is a great amount f *interpretation* in the Biblical narratives, that Jesus ppears to us there as seen by the eyes of love and ommitment. But is there some material that is objec-ive and free from devotional bias? The quest for this naterial is a very precise piece of surgery undertaken vith the utmost care to sterilize our instruments.

Where does the Christology that shall follow here npinge upon the attempt (if we may change our meta-hor) to pluck the naked Jesus from the robes of Biblical doration?

The attempt to elicit an uninterpretative picture of esus from the New Testament is warmly to be ap-lauded both for the fascinating, although certainly neager, results it may obtain, and for the intrinsic in-erest of the process, which demands the persistence nd subtlety of a Sherlock Holmes. Yet it is a work of ess than decisive importance for us. If we were trying o recapture for ourselves the experience, the "state of nind" of Jesus at some stage of his career, if we were ent upon duplicating within ourselves his emotional, spiritual, or intellectual condition (as, indeed, some nineteenth-century liberals urged us to do), it would obviously be a very critical matter to recover his own words and to see glimpses, at least, of him in character istic action so that we might infer something about his subjectivity. But the Central Generating Experience of Christianity is not Jesus' experience but that experi ence *of* Jesus *as the Christ* which the disciples de scribed. This means that the New Testament, repre senting as it does the attempts of men to discuss the first instances of the experience we seek, is the proper source *as it stands* for our work. Its "interpretative" quality is not a disadvantage to us, but is exactly what we need to study and respond to.

Form-critical disclosures of authentic historical ele ments in the New Testament are, then, of high value but not indispensable. They help us to see him to whose meaning for us the earliest Christians were trying to awaken us. Yet it is not a matter of much disappoint ment that what can thus be rescued from the Gospels and other sources is so slight. We may not know (and I think, do not know) more than that Jesus was baptized and crucified, and that between these two events he spoke with remarkable authority and colorful imagery about a "Kingdom of God," meaning the activity and power of God in the world, loving, judging, and forgiv ing people. He spoke of God's royal activity as present already in his time, and he spoke of it as reaching a climax, a fulfillment in the future. He demanded a ver dict; he called upon men to "repent," and thus to re spond to the Kingdom. That is, as they experienced the love and forgiveness of God and discovered themselves to be his joyful subjects, so they were to live love and forgiveness.

Perhaps we shall never be able to say more than this about the unquestionable teaching of Jesus. Perhaps even this is too much! But whatever slender resource we find will be enough. What matters is not that we should have a detailed photograph or psychograph of Jesus and a record of his teaching made eternally available through the genius of the Sony Corporation, but that the New Testament presents to us the effort of Christians to verbalize their experience of him who taught these things and performed or suffered the events. *The supremely critical thing, calling for our verdict today, is the fact that for those first Christians Jesus himself came to be seen as the focus or even the embodiment of the continuing activity by which God loves, judges, and forgives.*

Thus, in the pages of the New Testament we are exposed to the awakening of the disciples. Through their eyes we see Jesus and we "feel" their response to what they saw.

What sort of man was this Nazarene? Did he, for instance, really have the power to walk on water? Frankly, some of us may doubt it. But what is important is that *in that time and place,* with its presuppositions, Jesus was the kind of person of whom such a story could seriously be told. In our day the tale may become an embarrassment if we are asked to affirm its factuality, but that is simply not the point. We must ask what it means that such things are said of him, rather than whether they are "history" or mere legend.

It seems clear, then, that the early Christians resorted in good faith to various forms of imagery—using images current and communicative in their milieu but not necessarily in ours—in the attempt to affirm that Jesus of Nazareth was the decisive moment and event

in the history of the world (that is, of *this* world, whatever may be true of others). The images they used included some that sound strange to us now: "Son of
Man," "Son of God," "Messiah," and so on. We must not
be offended or discouraged by these thought forms
echoing dimly from another day; rather, we must try to
capture their meaning and express them in other images. It is precisely this that we shall now try to do by
means of the form of personal logic.

With this preamble we are ready to begin our sketch
of a dialogical Christology. Let us be clear that we shall
not be trying to "prove" that Jesus is the Christ, but we
shall be showing what it means to say that he is.

What is a saint? In popular thought a saint is a "godly"
person, and this means a person whose character is
shaped by the presence, the influence, of God. In dialogical terms, a saint is one whose humanity (the formal
contraplete) may be said to be shaped or structured by
the divine. In more familiar language he or she is a
person "in" whom God dwells, and the Spirit of God
influencing his motivation and behavior is there not to
rob him of humanity but to enable him to attain the
greatest heights of personhood.

Had they been willing only to claim sainthood of this
kind for their leader, the disciples and their first sup-
porters might have had an easier time. What they did
claim, however, was an absurdity to Hellenistic thought
and a scandal to the Hebrew. Jesus, they said, was not
like other men. There was a qualitative difference
about his life. Yet he *was* a man. He was a man as the
ancient prophets had been men, but he was a man
unlike any who had lived before or any who could live
again. Unwilling to deny his true humanity, the first
Christians nevertheless found themselves speaking as if

in Jesus God had somehow been uniquely present. A
modern theologian has tried to state their claim in
these vigorous words:

> It was by men that God gave Himself to men, till, in the
> fullness of time, He came, for good and all, in the God-
> man Christ, the living Word; in whom God was present,
> reconciling the world unto Himself, not merely acting
> through Him but present in Him. . . . He acted not only
> through Christ but in Christ.[19]

Is it any wonder that many a wise man, from the first
century to this, has found this assertion objectionable?
Hellenists of the first century were familiar with an-
thropomorphic deities, with divine redeemer-figures
and the like, but to impute authentic humanity to these
was quite another matter. On the other hand, Jewish
thought dealt comfortably with the idea of men whom
God chose, appointed to a task, and inspired; but such
men were entirely human. In our own time people find
little trouble with the concept of a great ethical
teacher, a charismatic leader (of whom we have a lamentable surplus on the religious scene but a disastrous
lack on the political), or a mystic. The romantically religious even accept cheerfully the idea of multiple divine
incarnations such as the avatars of Vishnu. But that
God, the limitlessly Real, the Eternal, should appear
enfleshed *once and necessarily only once,* that in an
improbable land at a particular and now remote epoch
there should be a Presence who was both divine and
human and no mere ambiguous mixture but entirely
both—to ancient and modern people alike such an idea
is often virtually unintelligible.

Many individuals, influenced deeply by the spirit of
Jesus, have been proud to call themselves Christians

but have wanted to stop short of affirming the complex divine and human character for him that we have been discussing. Sensitivity rebels against the Jesus cults of naïve, romantic Christianity, cults that identify Jesus so simply with God that his prayers become inexplicable, his temptations unreal, his humanity a sham. H. Richard Niebuhr tried to strike a middle course when he warned against the confusions that arise "when the proposition that Jesus Christ is God is converted into the proposition that God is Jesus Christ."[20] But is this only hair-splitting? Short of pantheism, on what grounds can the claim be made that Jesus Christ is God?

It is here that personal logic comes to the aid of the harassed but vital doctrine of the incarnation, the "becoming flesh" of the divine. Indeed, it may be said that the incarnation of God in the Christ is the single supreme and necessary paradigm of personal logic, revealing the fact that existence itself bears the structure of such logic.

What the New Testament Christians were struggling to say, I believe, is that Jesus had emerged as their Christ precisely because in him they had met the supreme Reality of this and every world enfleshed in a particular human life. If that claim can become more than so many words for us, it may invite our ridicule or it may become the point on which our minds break open to a new "seeing" of the world. To call Jesus "the Christ" is to say that if we truly see him, we are struck by an unprecedented awareness and shaken out of our routine patterns of thought. In him Reality itself is suddenly disclosing itself to us, and the importance or meaning of the world assumes a wholly new and astonishing dimension.

But precisely what did the New Testament Christians say about their leader? Having sampled an important strand of their teaching, we shall try to see it in the terms of personal logic.

One of the richest of New Testament Christologies is that contained in the first chapter of John's Gospel, where the Greek word *logos* is used repeatedly as a means of uncovering the eternal meaning of the Christ. To understand what is being said there we must have some feeling for the breadth and depth of the splendid word *logos,* for it is not really a word at all but a veritable treasure chest loaded to the brim with luminosity.

Logos, as is well known to most students of the Bible, means "word." Certainly it does mean "word," but what a tame, denatured rendering of *logos* that is! A *logos* may indeed be a vehicle of communication between two persons, but beyond communication it may be a means of *communion,* of genuine relatedness—not merely a "knowing about" one another but a profound "at-onement."

Further, *logos* may mean a purpose one has, and it may be that act or word in which one discloses this purpose. Above all, one's *logos* may be one's self-expression, as this is presented in words, in actions, in creativity or in anything else: it is one's own "meaning" being disclosed through purposive action.

Now we are ready to appreciate what John is trying to tell us in his opening chapter:

> When all things began, the Word *(logos)* already was. The Word dwelt with God, and what God was, the Word was. (John 1:1, NEB)

John is saying here that God's purposive, self-expressive creativity is *always* existent. It did not come into being as a sudden impulse, so that one day God said,

Why don't I make a universe? To be God is to be pur-
posively and self-expressively creative: that is what
John has to say, and he presses home the point:

> The Word, then, was with God at the beginning, and
> through him all things came to be. (John 1:2, NEB)

Now comes a further development of the theme. We
are told that

> All that came to be was alive with his life, and that life
> was the light of men. (John 1:4, NEB)

In other words, the life of men and the "light" and
wisdom of mankind are expressions of the *logos,* or
creative self-expression, of God. We are purposive and
creative, we are self-expressive, because we participate
in the expressiveness of God. But to be creative is not
to be imitative: if we truly share in the power of
creativity that brings the universe into being, we must
ourselves be centers of intention, and that may mean
that we intend sometimes in distinction from and even
in alienation from God, even though he remains the
Ground and Power of our purposing. In more conventional language, the very fact that we participate in the
creativity that is God's nature makes real the possibility
of our sin or estranging selfishness.

Since this is so, the *logos* of God is not merely innova-
tive in its creativity but, when it must be, it is re-
creative. That is, it is also the word or act of restoration
of that which has lost its way; it is the reaching out of
a will-to-communion:

> He (the *logos*) was in the world; but the world, though
> it owed its being to him, did not recognize him. . . . But
> to all who did receive him, to those who have yielded
> him their allegiance, he gave the right to become chil-
> dren of God. (John 1:10–12, NEB)

So God pervades the universe as the creative power that moves it, but he is also present in the domain of human consciousness as the impulse to find again our centeredness and purposiveness, not in alienating self-ishness but in our continuity with inclusive Reality, with that Source which, we recognize, makes brothers of all men. This power, this impulse, is certainly present among us and makes itself felt on occasion, but the individual will to power seems too strong for it; again and again we assert ourselves as centers of value against all others, we isolate ourselves in actions and attitudes that exploit or merely ignore others. We are the product and the very expression of God's *logos*, but we fail to recognize its impulse as what it is, and consequently we reject it. But that, says John, is not the end of the story:

> So the Word became flesh; he came to dwell among us, and we saw his glory. (John 1:14, NEB)

Here is the critical verse for our present purpose, for to understand this we must plunge into personal logic without restraint. The Fourth Gospel is telling us that at a particular historical moment the ever-present *logos* of God found itself in a concrete, singular life, and that this life and no other is the "Christ," the focus of God's self-disclosure and his purposiveness for and in the universe.

This climax of God's self-presentation can occur only once, as we learn in various places in the New Testament (cf. I Peter 3:18; Heb. 7:27 and 10:10; Rom. 6:10), and it is unique as the occurrence of the perfect and complete presence of the infinite God within the compass of a human life. As Paul declares, "it is in Christ that the complete being of the Godhead dwells embodied" (Col. 2:9, NEB).

So we have the teaching of the New Testament that the Christ is the unique embodiment of the purposive, restorative, creative self-expression of God and his will for communion with his creation. This is a splendidly succinct summary of something early Christians were trying to report concerning their experience. Unfortunately it is also nearly unintelligible! What, really, does it mean? Here we cast ourselves into dialogic.

The Personal Logic of Christhood

"Jesus" and "Christ" are contrapletal terms. "Christ" is the name of the act of God by which he emerges from the anonymity of universal Being and stands as visible, singular entity. In doing so, he affirms and patently envalues particularity, for it is in a finite and quite single entity that the Comprehensive has disclosed itself in action. On the other hand, "Jesus" is a personal name; but more than this, it is the name of that human being whose life was the structural pole of God's Christ-appearing. Jesus is the vehicle of God's act, he is the instrument of what God does; but he is even allowed to be that particular earthiness which shapes in its details the decisive action of God!

Let no one miss what is being said here. Had it been some other person who served as the locus of God's acting, the shape of the act would have been different even though its function, its intention, would have been the same. Another person might have caused the act to occur in a different milieu, to make use of different words, ideas, and events, and to reach a different climax. The *meaning* and *value* of the act would have been the same, but the circumstances would have been different.

In the New Testament we have discrepancies in different accounts of the same events. Thus, for example, in telling about the resurrection of Jesus, Matthew says that the first persons to know about this were Mary of Magdala and "the other Mary," for they had gone to the tomb and were confronted there by the absence of the expected body and by the presence of a most unexpected figure—an "angel" (or messenger of God). As they left the tomb they both met Jesus himself. Now, Mark's account agrees substantially with this, but he adds Salome to the number of women to whom these things happened and then suggests that, of the three, it was only Mary of Magdala who actually *saw* Jesus himself. Luke says that it was the two Marys and Joanna who went to the tomb, and that they saw not one but two messengers. The Fourth Gospel offers its own variations. The point here is that the significance of the stories remains the same—the unconquerable power of the Christ-act of God; but the shape of the stories varies with different witnesses. Those who think that words about God are the things that really matter cannot help being dismayed at such discrepancies and must stretch their ingenuity to explain them into oblivion. But God does not operate according to our prescriptions. The humanity of those in whom he works is not violated, and this means that their creativity may express itself even as error, but it is through their creativity that he works. Similarly, in electing to act by means of the life of Jesus he does not cancel the real humanity of Jesus, but allows the *man* to shape the details of the divine acting—the where, when, and how of it—while the *why* remains his own.

Jesus was known by his friends as a man. When tired, he slept; when discouraged, he prayed; when hungry and thirsty, he ate and drank (so much so, in fact, that detractors, used to more ethereal saints and gurus, were scandalized and, as Luke tells us in ch. 7:34, called him a glutton and a drinker!). His ideas were presented with charming clarity as a rule, with humanness, and even with occasional humor and irony; but they were not especially original. Most (if not all) of the sayings attributed to him can be found in other sources of his time or earlier. He was human. No doubt of it. His disciples were probably first attracted to him as a remarkable and authoritative, if unconventional, sort of saint.

When the time came, however, that his followers began to talk about Jesus in the strange terms of Christhood, of divine "Sonship" and so on, they were reporting that what they found in this saint was something altogether out of the ordinary, even for saints. They were reporting that his life had transmitted to them an inimitable Presence of God, and that it continued to do so despite his ignominious death as a criminal. They were affirming that they had found, and were still finding, themselves in the path of a movement, an acting of the Real, a *doing* by the Creative Source of all things. To call Jesus their Christ meant no less than that God himself had been discovered in action, with Jesus the skeleton of that action-presence.

God had moved within time and space, and this particular movement is named "Christ." Jesus is the structural contraplete of this Christ-act, and his is the life that structured it, so that while it expressed an eternal process and intention, its precise shape was as it was because of this particular piece of humanity that bore it.

If we may refer once again to our celebrated wheel,

we may say that the rim represents the Christ, the act in which the creative-restoring process of God in the universe becomes particularity. The hub represents Jesus of Nazareth, whose form (i.e., his personality, habits, characteristics, and propensities) prescribes the actual, existential shape of that particularity. In fact, Jesus of Nazareth particularizes the Christ in this unique form.

"Jesus Christ," then, is not just a name and a title, but a wonderfully rich composite term. If we are to preserve the meaning given it in Christian scripture, we must take great care not to allow our contrapletes to exchange positions. It is the divine that is the formal polarity; it is the divine act that is the supremely decisive element impinging upon our world and us. If we lose sight of this and allow Jesus—the human element —to become the formal one, so that the Christhood becomes the structural element, we are virtually back with the familiar idea of a saint: that is, a person whose character and behavior are influenced by his sensitivity to the presence of God. Yet even this is not quite correct, for the appropriate term for the divine contraplete within sainthood is not "Christ," since "Christ" has too restricted a meaning.

We begin to see a beautifully consistent picture. God, the Reality that is creative—because it *must* be continuously creative in fulfillment of its essence or character—brings (within itself) particularity to fruition. *God is, therefore, the Being or Reality of difference as much as of identity!* Let us savor that, for it is a truth that half the religious traditions of the world try to avoid. God treasures distinctions, uniqueness, the unrepeatable. No moment of history, therefore, shall ever come again, although there may be many that resemble one an-

other. The many finite *ones* exist—and really exist—
within the eternal One as beings of his Being. God loves
them, values them, preserves them, and wishes to fulfill
them in their various unique potentialities. This trea-
suring of the finite is, as it *must* be, itself made finitely
actual by the presence of the divine act within a single
and unrepeatable life.

Magnificent! Who would have thought of such a
thing! But when it has happened and we really see it,
we are forced into laughter and exclaim: "Of course!
What else?"

But are we just playing with words? Words can be our
masters, or they can be true *logoi*, vehicles of communication and communion. We are trying to find
words that shall convey an experience, for that is always
the legitimate task of theology. Perhaps we should, for
a moment, resort to some words that may conjure up
a picture for us, for the sake of those of us whose imagi-
nations work better that way.

Imagine a large sphere, the inside wall of which is
actually a set of mirrors. (Thus if one were inside this
sphere, he would see himself reflected by each mirror,
so that whichever way he turned, there would be his
image.) Now imagine further that a much smaller
sphere is suspended inside the other. It is something
like a tennis ball whose *outside* has been coated with a
reflective substance. This small sphere now bears upon
itself the images of all the separate mirrors that com-
prise the inside wall of the large sphere. These are all,
in a sense, *there* on its surface. Therefore among the
separate, particular mirrors we have described, this
small sphere is unique. Though in one sense it is just
another particular mirror, in another sense it is also the
entire large sphere (i.e., in the sense that it bears the
image of the entire upon itself).

Our picture fails us. Analogies are always brittle, and this one is especially so, but if we can be gentle with it, and a little generous, we may find in it a sort of visual representation of what we have been saying about the Christ. He is a particular man among others, but his uniqueness is that he alone bears the living presence of that Being, that Unity, that Reality which embraces all particulars. In order that he may really affirm particularity he can himself appear only *once* within history, for to appear twice or more times would negate his affirmation of singularity, and he would therefore no longer be *this* Word, this Christ, at all.

The Christ, of course (unlike our coated tennis ball), is not merely the reflection but the presence-in-act of the divine Reality appearing within the realm of its own finite particulars and given its actual shape by the human life that bore it.

Can one not now see a new light on some vexed and vexing questions of classical Christology? For instance, how many earnest partisans have split hairs (or even heads) over the question of whether Jesus was or was not "born of a virgin"? How many bad jokes have been conceived in very unvirginal minds by this question! But may it not be that stories surrounding the birth of our Lord may be largely untrue as applied to Jesus but profoundly true concerning the Christ? This means that Jesus may have been quite naturally and properly conceived, but the Christ for whom he was to become the vehicle was certainly brought into existence through no act of man but by the intention of God alone —he was, in fact, the concretion of God's enduring intention for the reconciliation of mankind to himself. This, I suggest, is the only important truth being affirmed by the story of a virgin birth, but in that story it is offered to us in the symbolic terms available to

Luke. Was the resurrected body of Jesus actually taken, at the end, into the sky on a cloud (as Luke depicts the scene)? Perhaps not (why must it be supposed that Gospel writers are dull fellows, devoid of creative imagination?); but the Christ, the divine act of invitation to mankind, is eternally present in God even after the moment of its temporal concretion in Palestine is ended. This act cannot be confined in a tomb! To put it baldly, the Christ is risen, regardless of what became of the body of Jesus.

Here, then, is the outline of a way of seeing Jesus as the Christ. He is by no means merely a good man, but is the necessarily single point of convergence of the universal and the concrete. Because God is in this particularity, all beings are envalued; and because this person, Jesus, shapes the universal's act, it has the form we see in the Gospels.

But more: Jesus is reported to have said, "My Father has never yet ceased his work" (John 5:17, NEB). This is another way of saying that creativity, issuing from love, is the abiding character of Reality. And as we confront Jesus' way of expressing this we are forced to recognize a truth that only revelation could have disclosed: it is not enough to think of God in such terms as Being/Becoming or Unity/Particularity. If we are to approach tentatively an understanding of what the word "God" should mean, we must reckon with its referent being supremely *active*, and that means that he is *Agent*. He works. He acts with meaning and intention. Therefore he is, indeed, all that Agency as we have discussed it entails. Properly speaking, he is Agent/Subject, and we see at once another facet of what it means to say that he created us in his own image: our Agency and its contrapletal Subjecthood are expressions of his, are the "image" of his!

Now, to the illumined eye, the entire universe has appeared as a splendor of Self-fulfilling action in which we are all participants!

Important implications for the value and meaning of life radiate from this vision of the Christ, and there is no end of them until we reach the end of meaning itself. Perhaps it will throw a little more light on our understanding of the Christ if we begin to explore the nearest of these implications.

CHAPTER 8

Avenues

So far we have moved from a discussion of God to a discussion of the Christ, and we have seen that for dialogical theology these are closely interwoven subjects. The Christ is an indispensable disclosure of God; in fact, a dialogical discussion of God may be said to call for a Christ.

In the present chapter we shall open for reflection several topics that derive their content directly from things already said, but we shall not attempt any exhaustive argument here. Rather, we shall simply be asking what difference might be made to one's practical involvement in life, to one's stance toward the world, if one took seriously the idea of Christ and the reality of his emergence in the world.

I. The ONE and the Ones

People are curiously ambivalent about uniqueness. On the one hand, every collector dreams of owning a postage stamp, a diamond, or an automobile that has never been and can never be duplicated. On the other hand, we look askance at atypical or uncharacteristic behavior.

In some measure our discomfort with some kinds of unrepeatable or at least unrepeated event or thing is probably reinforced by the climate of a more or less "scientific" age, for science is concerned with what can be generalized and expressed as "law," and with the experiment that reliably reproduces identical results whenever performed.

But this proper interest in the regular occasionally bedevils us by invading areas where it belongs, if at all, only with restraint. Thus it is quite appropriate for experimental psychology to deal in generalizations, but it is surely lamentable when this practice and preoccupation give rise to a form of "therapy" that fails to take seriously the personal distinctiveness of those whom it would cure. Again, educational psychology may usefully recognize some generalizations about development and maturation, but when a single child is expected to conform to some pattern of growth and behavior and, failing to do so, is automatically subjected to batteries of tests, we are in grave danger of convincing him that he is defective when he is only different. As many a college instructor can testify, by the time a child who has been victimized too often by this arrogant penchant for testing during his elementary and secondary school career reaches college, he is all too likely to have learned to discover his own idiosyncrasies with alarm and to conceal with shame his own most creative impulses.

For anyone who has been awakened to the Christhood of Jesus, however, the unique can never be lost in the mass. Whether as therapist or educator he can no longer be preoccupied with what is "normal" in general, but he seeks with serious concern to know what may be proper for this one person. To do this does not make his work easier, because treating persons as individuals and awaiting with some humility the disclosure of their authentic centeredness (instead of forcing them through a sieve that strains out the data we want to find and lets the rest be ignored) makes it hard to construct with them Utopias or even idyllic school programs. But he recognizes that uniqueness is made sacred by the unique manifestation in Christ of that Mystery which is the divine Center of Being and Value.

If the singular reality of others is important, so is that of oneself. Many people in our troubled time wander in psychological disarray until they learn, probably from an imported and charismatic purveyor of exotic religion, that they can find peace through forsaking their own authenticity and finite identity, and through learning instead to think themselves identical with a Cosmic Mind or something of the sort. This is sad, and points to a genuine dilemma facing many today: how to endure the fragility of their stark selfhood, so small in a world so vast, so weak amid forces and dangers so strong.

No one should underrate the risk involved in choosing to be oneself and to affirm oneself courageously with all one's mind and will. It is no parlor game to stand on the narrow ground of one's integrity and face the assaults of disease, defeat, and disaster; one soon realizes that he spoke well who said, "It is not dying that is hard; it is living that defeats us."

But the Christian has seen the envaluing of the individual in the Christ, and he knows that the basic ethical law of his Faith is, "You shall love your neighbor as yourself" (Matt. 22:39), which implies as much the love of himself as of his neighbor. His question, then, is not how to abandon himself in order to love the other, but how so to love himself that he can also love the other, and thereby promote the fulfillment of both.

All this means that no Christian can submit to the illusion that his or anyone's destiny lies in the loss of personhood, of individual integrity, of centered awareness which entails both the awareness of oneself as this particular self, and the awareness of others as quite other. He does not confuse spiritual maturity with the facelessness of uniform behavior or the sickly sweetness of a bloodless and ascetic pietism. Rather, he recognizes himself as called to fullness of life in the enjoyment, so far as is possible, of all that God has made, and called also to help others achieve that fullness.

God is the One whose power to be is intrinsic; but this manner of being involves the dependent reality of the *ones* he calls into existence, and they serve him and love him best who serve and love each other.

But here, again, the Christian finds his dialogical vision of the God he worships intruding upon his understanding. There is an immediate response in most people to such phrases as "love of mankind" and "universal brotherhood." The Christian would like to melt beneath the sunshine of these words, too, but finds that he cannot. Indeed, he recognizes them as sham and impudent pretense. He is not called by his God to love "mankind" although this is very easy to do. It is easy to do because "mankind" is an abstraction without blood or muscle, and all those other sweet, inclusive phrases are no better. No, it is not to love mankind but to love *that one* in all his dreadful angularity, his uncomfortable and embarrassingly abrasive particularity, that the Christian (perhaps reluctantly) knows himself commanded.

Love, of course, in this context is not sentimentality but an openness to the other of the kind discussed earlier, and it issues in practical service. How often have we seen congregations that prided themselves on their

"Christian fellowship" simply because they had mastered the art of continuously smiling. In such churches one entered the door and was struck by a wide-eyed and almost breathless welcome; one sat in a pew and evoked instant smiles from all sides; one listened to a sermon by a gentleman who might have been demonstrating the effectiveness of his dental adhesive; even the choir performed like a forest of teeth. But one could look in vain for evidence that any of these people spent an ounce of energy per week on really confronting the immediate and inconvenient need of a single human being. By contrast, consider the example of a small Methodist church in an Australian suburb with the enigmatic name Dee Why. The young and energetic minister of this church does not conceive of his task as simply meeting the spiritual or emotional needs of the members of his congregation. He considers himself responsible for facilitating *their* ministry to the community, and such is his vision and theirs that it is not only the large-scale, dramatic social welfare program that concerns them. They are serious about confronting in love the actual and unromantic needs of the most inconspicuous individuals. Thus, various members of the congregation, together with their minister, sometimes at very considerable inconvenience to themselves, have for many months faithfully arrived each day to help a man, old now and ill, to prepare for bed and finally to settle into it. No luster attaches to this, and more often than not the man they are helping does not even recognize them. To do this once or twice would not be remarkable. But for people to accept joyfully the task of caring, over an indefinite period that may stretch into years, for a man who can, in return, offer them nothing but his need—this is love.

The unity of Being, of God, is a profound and basic truth, but it is no less the truth that you and I are created to be individuals within that unity and to preserve in ourselves and to support in each other what it has been given us to be. Indeed, we may say that sin consists very largely of neglecting those needs in ourselves and in others which relate to personal growth. The failure to meet such needs leads to the diminishment of our individual authenticity and fulfillment.

What we are saying here must not be diluted. It is fashionable in many quarters today to commend various disciplines of meditation in which people find relief from anxiety or tension by temporarily losing the awareness of the separation of self and other. No one need doubt that such disciplines can work or that it is restful to cleanse one's mind of discordant multiplicity and have it settle quietly in the sense of simplicity and nondiscrimination. Such experiences are beneficial for many people at times of tension. But the Christian must know that they can become as destructive as any other form of self-indulgence. It is the ultimate spiritual arrogance, however much disguised by the cloak of humility, when any one of us actually uses such a method to overcome the risk of individuality; when, for instance, we try to meditate our fellows and ourselves out of the sometimes painful privilege of our endowed particularity and into a spurious sense of cosmic oneness. Those who do this are not simply self-deceived: they are refusing to move willingly within the stream of God's acting through the world; they are actually almost declining to be real!

A master of great meditational power once sat naked on the ground and, closing his eyes and restraining all his senses, turned his thoughts inward to their source until consciousness of all objects had passed from his mind. He entered successively all the stages of trance until, in a state of absolute objectless awareness, he rested in perfect tranquillity beyond either sorrow or joy.

This went on for a very long time. Meanwhile, a tiny seed in the ground beneath the master germinated and thrust upward a green finger. Encountering opposition, the shoot explored until it found a point of least resistance and began a Herculean climb through the bowels and intestines of the man entranced. At last it thrust a tentative tip through the lips, which were slightly opened in an enigmatic smile.

At this moment the man emerged from his rapture and, noting the plant, was delighted.

"Welcome," he said. "You and I are the perfect illustration of the most enormous truth the world can know, for we are obviously one, with no distinction between us!" And he slightly shifted his position.

"No doubt," said the plant, "but meanwhile please don't move again or I'm done for."

"We point to the unity of all that is," said the man. "We are a living symbol to the world of the eternal and changeless oneness of Reality in which all seeming difference is mere untruth."

"All right," replied the plant, "but do you mind if we don't talk?"

"Ah," said the master gently, "even you, my little friend and my very self, have realized that to keep silence is the only way to express the highest Truth."

"Not really," the plant answered, "but I've certainly realized that to keep silence is the only way to avoid being chewed."

Thus Christianity walks between simple pluralism and simple non-dualism or monism. Its dialogical mode of thought—derived from and serving to interpret its Central Generating Experience—helps it to see that the reality of the One who is the indivisible God and the reality of the ones who are the separate existents of daily experience are not mutually exclusive but are fulfilled only in their relation to each other. Seeing this, the Christian's life is changed. In any given moment he may behave exactly like thousands of others—enjoying his food, laughing with his friends, weeping for those he loves, and seeking the good of others and of himself. But the total structure of his living is made consistent by the distinctive way he views Reality and all that expresses it.

II. Eternity and Time

There are people who become infatuated with eternity and find nothing so delightful as the prospect of an "eternal now" in which nothing really moves or happens because there is no real "there" and no real "thence" between which motion might occur. Others find such an image depressing, and the very possibility of eternal life becoming theirs arouses only the anticipation of timeless boredom.

The phrase "eternal life," so dear to the Fourth Gospel, immediately raises a problem for us quite apart from what we may think such a thing might "feel" like. If our human minds can only vaguely grasp the idea of eternity, of timelessness, we can hardly be expected to make sense of it when it is associated with "life." Life is motion, it entails growth and change. It is a thing of sequences and explorations. How, then, can life ever be timeless—since time is the distance between events and eternity must be simply the absence of any events?

Surely "life" and "eternal" are mutually exclusive terms. Life and time belong together, but eternity can only be lifeless.

The lesson to be learned from the appearance among us of the Christ is that eternity, in its literal sense, cannot appropriately be applied to God after all. The Christ is Reality acting within time and stamping upon all our moments the mark of significance. As such, he is also the message that time is not alien to Reality; as moments are real, so time as a flow has its being within Being. Time is contrapletal to the transtemporality of God, and "eternity" can be meaningfully applied to God only if it is modified, shaped by our understanding of time as its structural contraplete.

What we are trying to say here is that Reality is not an absolute stillness, it is not static. As we said earlier, the very presence of a world and of time declares that Being is Being/Becoming and has its perfection not as something lifeless and immobile but as a dynamic process. Eternity/Time is the mode of Reality, for the Real (yes, God himself) is progressively shaped by the processes of time and history. But "eternity" may be an unfortunate term for us to use, impossible even to modify properly so that it can find its place in our logic. It is useful if it points to the fact that Reality transcends the limitations of events in time, i.e., that Reality cannot be imprisoned in the succession of moments which contains us. But it is inappropriate if it suggests that Reality is stolid and unprogressive, literally lifeless. Perhaps, rather than speaking of Eternity as the contraplete of Time, we should find another term. "Supraternity"—cacophonous though it be—may serve us better. Supraternity/Time: this is the milieu of God as the Christ discloses it through his presence among us.

We have now argued for a way of thinking about God
that many classical theists and their contemporary followers would find quite unacceptable. They suppose
that God, being perfect, must be unchanging. When
Scripture says of Christ that he is "the same yesterday
and today and for ever," they suppose that it means this
in an ontological sense, and that there can be no responsiveness in God, for motion of any kind is an imperfec-
tion.

What a strange idea that is in a world like ours! A fond
parent may think his three-year-old child is "perfect,"
but he will not continue to think this of the child if at
the age of ten it still looks, sounds, and acts as it did at
three! Perfection is not static. On the contrary, perfection is being what one should be at a given time, and
if God is perfect, this is the mode of his perfection.
Since it is the character of God to create, he would be
imperfect if he were uncreative and thus unchanging.
Since love is his nature, he would be less than perfect
if he did not love—i.e., cherish and seek the fulfillment
of—whatever his creativity brings into being. This,
after all, is why the Christ-act must be the consummation of his creativity, for it is the act by which he invites
to fulfillment that which has become estranged and
disordered. This is why Christians speak of a "Trinity"
when they discuss God, and why they include the idea
of the Holy Spirit in their way of talking about him. The
Spirit is a way of God's being continually creative: the
term refers to his unbroken presence among and
within us as an impulse to reconciliation with each
other and with God himself.

So the Christ, understood dialogically, breaks the
confining illusion of lifeless eternity and static perfection and allows God to be seen as the continually

fulfilled and fulfilling Reality moving in us all. The Christ gathers all events, good and bad, and makes of them a progress that—since the human participants in it participate in the creativity of God—is never simply extrinsically determined. Since all creativity is in continuity with God's, this progress is never out of control. It was a kindred idea that Whitehead developed intriguingly through his concept of the "primordial" and "consequent" natures of God.

The practical consequences of our view of things result from the sacralizing of life and its processes, which we now see as real. Mircea Eliade has pointed to the persistent tendency of religious persons to try to bring about the sanctification of our world by allowing it to be invaded by the realm or power of the divine. So our *time* is made sacred by the device of choosing a special moment, an occasion when the sacred can be brought into our stream and can thus make it all holy. Modern Christians usually elect Sunday morning as the sacred time through which the divine will penetrate and somehow sanctify their entire week. Space must also be made holy so that there may be sacred places through which all our territory is touched by God.[21]

For the dialogical Christian, however, God does not have to invade our world, for our world has its existence only within God. On the other hand, if there is a way in which we become more wholeheartedly involved in the sacralizing (or fulfilling) of human life, it is not through places and times but through processes. God moves creatively, and we who would fulfill human destiny must therefore find our God not chiefly in passivity (although, indeed, he is there to be found, too), but in activity, since this is the dominant mode of being in time. And especially do we find God in activity that participates in the movement toward wholeness,

health, and creativity in man and nature. To promote
the growth, therefore, of a single pine tree may be a
more sacred act than an hour of earnest "spiritual"
wrestling with one's own sense of guilt, egoism, or
weakness, for it is an act that leads us out of self-preoc-
cupation and into the process by which this world lives.

III. Spirit and Matter

Our reference above to the Holy Spirit of God suggests another area of thought in which our present theological formulations shed some light.

"Spirit" is a word of enormous importance to theological discussion, yet it is very difficult to define. Dic-
tionaries offer such alleged synonyms as "breath,"
"courage," "life," "vigor," and the like, or suggest that
it refers to the "life principle" (whatever that may
mean) or the conscious, thinking, feeling "part" of man.
This sort of statement is, however, interpretation
rather than definition and certainly does not do justice
to the many complex ways in which the word is used.
I want to suggest that whatever else it may mean in the
context of Christian discussion, "spirit" very impor-
tantly refers to a quality that is discoverable in life and
that cannot quite be reduced to material terms or to
any that lend themselves to measurement or experimental manipulation. People who believe that there is
nothing in human experience that cannot be quantified
will, of course, lose interest in our discussion and smil-
ingly consign us to the realm of the "spooky" and super-
stitious. But such an attitude is itself a kind of superstition—an irrational restriction of the data of our life to
arbitrarily approved instruments and whatever these
can discover.

Spirit is a sort of "presence" and a power of responsiveness, a sensitivity within us. To say that "God is spirit" (John 4:24) means at least that he is a living, responsive presence rather than an indifferent, mechanistic object. Thus, to go further and say that "those who worship him must worship in spirit" means that mere ritual, the performance of empty actions, the absentminded mouthing of words, is not worship. Presence must be met by presence, response by response.

Spirit is, therefore, a way of being what one is. Borrowing from Hellenists, however, Christians quite early advanced the cause of the strange idea that "spirit" was an entity of some kind that could be *isolated* from matter. Paul's admittedly ambiguous teaching about "spirit and flesh" was read as though he were a Greek rather than a Hebrew and as though he could believe that man had "a spirit," which was a sort of ethereal something imprisoned in his body.

Thus, in popular thought at least, spirit and matter became two substances, and there was an antipathy between them. Naturally this led to a despising of "the flesh" by the pious and to attempts by those who wanted to be "spiritual" to mitigate the power of their bodies. So asceticism was eagerly embraced by some, and the "mortification of the flesh" became the salubrious pastime of the faithful.

Now, spirit cannot be reduced to matter, but one wonders how the radical separation of spirit and matter could have been tolerated in a tradition that rested upon Jewish religious ideas of the unity of man (as a psychosomatic organism) and whose Central Generating Experience was an awakening to the meaning of an *incarnation*—the enfleshment of a divine act.

Let us be clear. "Spirit" is not, for classical Judaism or for authentic Christianity which has not lost its way in inappropriate philosophy, a rival stuff at enmity with matter. It is, as we have said, a way of being, whether we happen to consist of matter or not, and Jesus, the human contraplete of the divine Christ-act, was an instance of spiritual personhood.

Spirit is a way that matter (or matter-energy, or whatever else we decide to call the stuff of the universe) can sometimes express itself and be. To have understood this would have saved many an earnest Christian from an empty stomach, for it means that matter, including our bodies, is not an enemy to be beaten, nor even a thing of such little importance that it may be neglected. Matter is what we are. But we are matter that has the capacity to rise to the quality of being that we call spirit.

But can we say more about this "quality" of being? I think we can, and I think dialogic helps us to do so. Spirit functions in us as a contraplete, shaping our behavior and turning it toward responsiveness, sensitivity, and love. We are, as fully developed human beings, then, matter/spirit.

Surely this means that whatever we usually mean by "matter" is suddenly ennobled in our eyes. It is rich in value because it has the potential to rise to spiritual expression, and when it does it is the entire entity that must be respected, not merely the spiritual quality. Plainly, this means that there can be no truly Christian ethic that disparages matter. There can be no worthy "loving" of other persons simply in their spirituality. Rather, we must be concerned for the welfare of the whole person as a single matter/spirit entity, and we must never dismiss as unimportant the hunger and pain of the flesh. This must be said, unfortunately, because Christians have sometimes spoken as if "saving souls" were all that mattered, and religionists of some other stripes have cheerfully countenanced the destruction of bodies because the "spirit" survived and was utterly other than the flesh. Christians of the first century, and their Jewish neighbors, would generally have found such thinking intolerable. If the body died, they would have said, there was nothing to survive. "Spirit" or "soul" is a mode of being, not a "thing," and if God chooses to immortalize anyone he must do it by reconstituting or "resurrecting" them as some kind of physical entity. Even Paul is clear that unless the dead are "raised" they are very, very dead; there is no immortal something in them as part of their inherent being (cf. I Cor. 15:12–20).

Thus, we are matter/spirit and must be concerned about each other as such. Among Christians, one thinks of the "social gospel" movement as coming closest to emphasizing the importance of attending to and healing the material conditions of life as a religious duty. Yet even here, on occasion, there seems to have been a tendency not to see the continuity of flesh and spirit we have discovered. Programs of reform, one gathers, were sometimes justified by a few on the grounds that they led to a new religious sensitivity and appreciation in those who had been helped. But the giving of a cup of cold water to one who is thirsty is not justified only if the recipient then gets up to praise God; it is justified because it has remedied a lack in the order of things, it has sustained a body. It seems to me that a Marxist who had established a just economic order (if indeed he had) would be a better servant of the spirit than a monk who withdrew into introspective meditation and ignored the needs of the fleshy world, for it is as materially constituted beings that we are capable of spirit. Similarly, an economist who in these 1970's showed us how to curb inflation might actually achieve more for the Kingdom of God than Billy Graham!

On the other hand, matter that has the capacity to attain spirit and fails to do so is refusing its destiny. There are so many examples of this miserable failure about us that one may choose almost at random. In this, for instance, we see the saddest sin of much human sexuality. Our tragedy is not that so much sexual satisfaction occurs outside the legal bonds of marriage, but that inside or outside marriage so much of it is presenceless, unresponsive, exploitative, merely casual, and thus depersonalizing. There is lacking a profound mutual care that is spiritual. There is, alas, such a thing as coincidental rape (even between consenting adults!) and it occurs in "marriage" (if that word is used merely to mean legality) as much as outside it, for it occurs when two persons treat each other as instruments for the relief of sexual tension.

But if man can be described as spiritual matter or as matter/spirit, what shall we say of God? He who is our encompassing Reality must be Spirit whose structural contraplete is matter! This does not make God material, and therefore finite—but it does affirm that the Spirit who is God, choosing to embrace a material universe, is what he is because of that decision. Henceforth the Becoming of God is conditioned by events within the material realm that exists within him.

This means that in addition to Being/Becoming and Unity/Particularity, we must use the polarity Spirit/Matter in our thinking about God, and that, in turn, means that one of the ways by which we learn how to think about him is science.

Far from being at enmity with religion, science is a supremely religious enterprise. Whatever we can know about the order of things, about the character of the universe, is data for our thinking about God. Not because God can pantheistically be reduced to matter, but because the universe is a manner of God's being. Thus, one of the most important and exciting of recent theological statements is: $E = mc^2$.

When Christians recognized that God was continuously active within the universe (as the universe is continuously sustained within him) they expressed this understanding again in terms of spirit: the "Holy Spirit" became the name of the incessant action by which God moved, led, healed, and became a felt Presence in the world. And for us to become spiritual is to participate in those activities: not to abandon the world or belittle it, but ourselves to become responsive and healing presences to each other and to the entire natural and material order. Thus it may be seen that Christianity, as we understand it, can never be content with idealistic philosophy as the tool of its expression. It need not descend into crass materialism, either, but it recognizes idealism (in the metaphysical sense of the term) as the fruitless quest for a bloodless Reality.

IV. The Action of Embracing Trust

Our creative energies, bequeathed to us by God as necessary expressions of his own creativity and love, have made possible the self-centered estrangements we experience in our life with each other and with God himself. The cure for these estrangements cannot be the restraint of our power for initiative, for while the application of such restraint might bring about the end of our destructive actions, it would also render us no longer the vessels of the creative thrust that is part of the expression of God's Spirit in the world. The cure, then, must be a new initiative by God, one in which his creativity takes the form of a reconciling, healing action.

Moreover, God's work of healing cannot be completed in some gesture that fails to span the chasm of estrangement; it cannot be merely good advice, an encouraging word, or a splendid example, but it must be an actual bridge, the forging of a genuine link that holds together the divine, with its thrust toward harmony and fulfillment, and the human, with its ambiguities and frequent falling into harmfulness: nothing less will do in a world that is no mere Idea in the Cosmic Mind, but a participant in the divine *Reality.*

This means that a "word" will not suffice to overcome the terrible chasm whose dimensions are drawn for us every day in the newspaper's running account of cruelty, corruption, and despair. What we need is an action, and an action that is as much rooted in divinity as in humanity, an action that enters the sphere of alienation without leaving the sphere of love. We are like people caught in a whirlpool that they are ignorantly enjoying. We need, not a swimming lesson, but an entering of the vortex itself by him who would save us.

At once we see that Christologies that speak as if the Christ were merely a Word from God must fail. Of course he is a word, and through attending to the Christ as word much of our darkness and ignorance may be dispelled. But he is and must be more than that. In the Christ God does not merely tell us that we are caught and may be liberated, lost and may be found; in the Christ God is active in the whirlpool itself. Christ has bridged the gulf, for he is precisely that act of God which is embodied in humanity—in human form and flesh. He is that act of God which plunges into the hatred we generate for each other, and which yet remains in love.

The cross on which Jesus died and on which the Christ-act achieved its climax is a terrible instance of the estrangement of persons from each other and from God, but in submitting to this ignominy, Jesus brought the Christhood he bore to the most dramatically expressive moment of its career. The Presence of God participates in the Christ, and because of Jesus it is involved in a moment of suffered alienation. Yet it is never less than a dauntless will-to-reconciliation, epitomized as Jesus cried, "Father, forgive them" (Luke 23: 34). We are too familiar with two thousand years of clichés about the crucifixion for the drama of it to move us much anymore, but perhaps we can recover a little of the wonder we owe it if we think of it against a different and currently popular background.

Had Jesus been a kung fu master out to save the world with a band of carefully trained followers who commanded the martial arts, he might have either accepted or resisted crucifixion, but he would in any case have prepared himself long before it occurred to be "above" the situation. It is the genius of Christianity to recognize the inadequacy of that kind of thing. The profound reconciliation God seeks with us can be attained only in an act which includes such commitment to mankind that it rejects even the possibility of being inviolable. The Christ as an act of the divine expresses the *trust* with which God approaches us—a trust that knows full well it will be violated, but does not diminish itself by seeking power *over* the problem. Only such absolute and absolutely violated trust can be the adequate bridge, because it is utterly unaggressive (even to the point of being unprepared for defense), yet utterly unquenchable. It has remained *trust* to meet and counteract distrust; it has remained *love* without defensive qualifications under the strain of successful hostility.

When we speak of the "incarnation" of God in his Christ, then, we refer to a singular occurrence; the power that God is, expressed as helplessness in order to incorporate in a unique event the estrangement of mankind and the inclusive, unselective will-to-reconciliation of God. It is Being occurring as Particularity in order that the latter may give up trying to delude itself that it is itself purely Being (or God) and may find again its peace, its joy, and its confidence as Particularity embraced by Being. It is Being so acting that beings like ourselves may laugh at all our earthy or mystical pretensions and be content to be ourselves within him in whom we live and move.

If we respond to this divine act of Christ, we know ourselves to be limited, singular, vulnerable. But we find a ground in it for trusting Reality instead of trying to escape or monopolize Reality. And we go out to the risk of daily life knowing ourselves enveloped by that splendid trust with which God embraces us, impelled ourselves to offer trust in a trustless world, maybe to accept crucifixion (although in the sophisticated fashion of modern society), but always to be active for that which reconciles person to person, humanity to God, and man to nature.

CHAPTER 9

A
Few
Loose
Ends

A little boy had come home from Sunday school deeply preoccupied with a new theological idea. After ten minutes of unrewarding reflection he decided to seek an independent opinion, and as his mother was passing through the room he asked, "Mother, is God really everywhere?"

"Why yes, dear, he certainly is."

"Is he really right here in our town?"

"Indeed he is, son, right here in our street!"

"Well, is he in this house?"

"Of course he is, dear. Isn't that wonderful?"

"Is he in this room?"

"Yes, even in this very room."

A pause follows, while young eyes search out a suitable object. Then, "Is he even in this ink bottle?"

Maternal laughter, but an indulgent, "Yes, honey, he's even there."

Then, a sudden paroxysm of movement as small hands clap tightly down over the top of the bottle and a voice exults, "Got 'im!"

Of course we have not "got" him. Our words have been like arrows which, however straight the archer thought their flight, always fell short or turned aside from the target. No matter. It is enough that we have glimpsed a way of thinking about God and his Christ that opens our eyes to the wonder of the world in all its amazing multiplicity. It is a universe of mystery (and continues to be so, no matter how much we discover about it); it is an unfinished symphony in which there are sad and difficult passages as well as moments of lilting melody and glorious crescendo. For the universe is moving. God is shaping his future with the rough materials of time.

But how does one know all this? A simple question, deserving a direct answer. In fact, one doesn't know all this. No one "knows" anything about the meaning of what we are and what we experience, but people catch glimpses that seem to be light, and by them they study what appears to be a fragment of the pattern. At best, however, we see "only puzzling reflections in a mirror," as Paul says (I Cor. 13:12, NEB), and he who claims more on the basis of some intense experience or kind of consciousness is simply naïve about the functioning of subjectivity. Yet for some of us a moment has come that feels like an awakening; we saw something, and in its light many things fall into place. We felt a Presence beyond ourselves and also within us, and we were confident that we had been grasped by a meaning beyond our imagining. But are we merely deceived?

Perhaps. But no one can do more than to bring his intelligence and his experience together with his most seemingly luminous perceptions and to act in commitment to a consequent vision of truth. Yet this vision must be heuristic, not dogmatic; it must make him available for new discoveries and profounder understandings. And if this is a vision that leads him not to deny any part of his experience but to accept and order it all in a way that allows him to participate constructively in the flow of things, he is fortunate indeed. It is our conviction that the Christ, as we have seen him here, offers us just such a vision.

Can we, then, affirm our convictions without the

slightest shadow of doubt? Certainly not. To doubt is to be human, to be alive, and to acknowledge our finitude. To abandon doubt is not to achieve truth but to have fled from the knowledge that we and all our experience, however certain it has seemed, are fragments in a universe that transcends us. But doubt is a joyless thing only if it dominates our faith. If it becomes the flavor of our spirit, it may demolish us at last. Let it, then, be where it may serve us best: alive and well within our faith. There it may lead us to continue to question, to pursue understanding, to avoid fanaticism. But it will not immobilize us, for faith will be the dominant contraplete with which we cheerfully meet and embrace the world.

It is, after all, quite possible for me to doubt the existence of my wife. She may be only the figment of a disordered mind. But knowing her, I can constructively use my power of questioning and wondering so that it leads me to deeper and richer understanding and to profounder love of one who makes the world a better place for me. Doubt, thus, exists within faith not to decay it but to save it from shallow infatuation or from collapse into dull acceptance. It is to faith structured by doubt that the Christian is called by his vision.

Because faith/doubt is the backbone of the Christian's life, he listens to what other men report about their understandings. Sometimes he finds things to incorporate into his own, and sometimes he is disappointed to find nothing that can help him grow. But he does not only listen. He cares enough to declare his own convictions, even to argue for them, not despising other visions but convinced that no one has a monopoly on truth . . . or error!

The End . . . of the Beginning

Our discussion of dialogical theology has lasted about as long as one book may reasonably permit. To be sure, the subject has only been opened and there is much more ground to be explored. It would be possible, for instance, to show that such classical theological words as communion, reconciliation, community, mission, worship, and repentance are thoroughly dialogical, and their depth can only be penetrated if they are seen in dialogical form. That, however, must await another book.

Let it be sufficient for now that we have surveyed perfunctorily the beginnings of a Christian theology with the aid of personal logic. It is worth noting that whereas in some systems of thought one finds the Christ to be rather "stuck on" to God as a sort of dubious appendage, he is here recognized for what the disciples saw in him: an indispensable disclosure of God and a manifestation of God in action; a disclosure without which we cannot know all that it is good for us to know.

To see the world through eyes that have been opened to this Christ is to see it newly. To live in faithful obedience to him whose act the Christ was is to begin in joy to fashion one's life as a vehicle of relationship, of active service, of admiration and compassion for whatever has being. It is to be a person who attains spirit and is open to others, who looks at them and sees *them* rather than an image projected on them by one's own values and desires. It is to be one who knows that while faith without its structuring doubt is blindness, faith without its expression in action, in service, in living toward others is faith in something other than that creative Agent to whom Jesus Christ directed us.

Now, further to illuminate our image of the Christ and that Reality which he expressed, we shall add a final chapter in which dialogical Christianity shall be set in the context of two very impressive alternative visions.

CHAPTER 10

Being
and Particularity:
Christianity
Among World Religions

The river eddied and swirled its way through the remains of an old bridge until, out in the sun once more, it preened itself in slow, smooth elegance. Even the debris it carried seemed somehow to be held in an arrogance of ownership. And on a rock that leaned out over its prosperous stomach stood a solitary boy.

Brown, thin legs and arms flowed out from red shorts and a red and white striped shirt, and on top of a sober, freckled face lay a bird's nest of undisciplined hair. His eyes, almost china blue, were watchful and guarded, alive but offering little. The whole, small body was poised in concentration like a single eye fixed on the river or one great ear listening. He wondered:

"What's a river? Is it one whole thing, like a snake coiling across the countryside? Or is it really lots of things, lots of single drops of water rushing arm in arm toward the sea? Is the river the real thing, or just its separate drops? For that matter" (and here a new idea struck him with an almost physical force), "is anything out there real at all? Suppose I'm just dreaming the river; that would mean that when I stop thinking about it it doesn't exist any more. And when I die, the river dies too—no more flowing to the sea, no more fish, no more sand or mud. Maybe the whole world is just something I think. Maybe even I'm just something I think. If I stop thinking—stop thinking about anything at all—maybe everything would stop. Right there!"

A small smile curved his thin lips. The boy played for a moment with his new idea and enjoyed, for a moment, being master of the worlds, able to banish everything to the never-was with the stopping of a thought.

In a world of masques and fancies only the dullest mind has never asked about the character of reality: What *is?* Is the knower real? Is what he knows real? Or is only the knowing itself real? Or are all three equally real? If by "real" we mean *there,* regardless of anyone's knowing, is anything real at all?

We have seen that René Descartes felt that the reality of a knower (or thinker) was self-evident, and his problem was to justify his conviction that the objects apparently known by the thinker, including other thinkers, also existed. Here is the root of a persistent dilemma in philosophy. It seems "natural" or inevitable to begin our inquiry about the real with the confident affirmation of the experience of thinking or experiencing itself, making this a starting point for further exploration. That is, we commonly start from the ubiquitous experience of subjecthood and, whether we thereafter try to be idealists or realists or to escape the errors of both these alternatives, our entire metaphysical edifice is raised upon the foundation of our experience of being a subject.

As John Macmurray has shown, however, if we accept subjectivity (whether we call it "I think" or "I intuit" or "I know in mystical immediacy") as our unexamined starting point, we have already implicitly destroyed the bridge between subject and object. For subjectivity is, and must remain, only subjectivity—interior awareness which may include convictions about objects it "knows," but which can never in any way demonstrate their reality. Thereafter the problem of accounting for the appearance of an object becomes inescapable.

Two classic and influential answers to the question of the reality of subject and object are, first, to abandon the object and in some fashion to affirm only subjectivity; and, second, to abandon in some way the reality of the subject and to affirm objectivity. While these "answers" run into such difficulties that their effects tend, in practice, to be mitigated considerably, the world has seen interesting attempts to establish them. It is the contention of this book that a dialogical or act-centered understanding of central Christian perceptions, especially concerning the Christ, offers a luminous vantage point for the surveying and interpreting of life. To sharpen the distinctiveness of that perspective I propose now briefly to outline an example of each of the two great alternatives I have referred to in this paragraph, without attempting to do full justice to either.

Our exemplary instance of the idealistic abandonment of objects will be the Vedantic nondualism of Shankara, and our philosophy of objectivity will be the "realistic" pluralism of classical Theravada Buddhism. Let it be understood that a better case can be made for each of these positions than I will attempt here; they have sustained the hopes of good people for many centuries and I have no wish to belittle them, especially since I have felt powerfully the attraction of both. But they are in opposition to each other and to the position I have advanced, and it is that opposition which constitutes their interest and usefulness for us at present.

Shankara

The illustrious Shankara, saint and thinker of the late eighth century A.D., is not only the most influential single figure ever to appear on the intricate stage of Indian philosophy, but is also one of the most luminous exponents of what we may approximately call idealism to appear anywhere. His writing is, to a Westerner, tiresomely repetitive, and the questions he chooses to neglect are often just the ones a European or American would spend many pages discussing, but his work retains a charm that cannot escape a sensitive reader even today.

Shankara stood firmly in a strong Indian tradition that found in subjective inwardness the road to the deepest understanding of truth, and his philosophy is an attempt to present the implications of that subjectivity in as coherent and consistent a form as possible. In doing this he offers us a classic statement of a nondualism that stands in marked contrast to the teaching of the Buddha (as the latter is represented in the ancient Pali canon of the Theravada school) and to the dialogical realism we have outlined in this book. Let us examine some of the main lines of his thought.

The conclusion of Shankara's metaphysics is that truth or reality (which are the same) is neither two entities nor many. Ultimate Reality is "not-two." It is better, perhaps, not to say that it is *one,* for that might be a word too definite and therefore limiting to apply to reality. At any rate, a knower, the thing he knows, and the experience of knowing are identical in essence, and every distinction our senses seem to reveal to us between this and that, you and me, self and not-self, subject and object, and so on is no more than a peculiar sort of error. To the pragmatic Westerner this may seem to make no sense at all, so we must look more closely at what India's great sage is saying.

A major assumption of Shankara's philosophy is that *only that can be "real" or the "truth" in a final sense which never changes or ceases to exist.* Shankara applies to the world as a whole the sort of critique most of us reserve for things like mirages or optical illusions. We say that a mirage is real enough as a mirage, but that it is deceptive. It will not withstand close scrutiny, but finally dissolves to reveal the more substantial reality of the desert sand. For Shankara the world as we see it daily is like that. It has a kind of deceiving reality or presence, but if one sees "through" it, one discovers that all its shapes are empty of substance and that reality—which is beyond such categories as shape or substance—remains unchanging and eternal. Like a mirage, all that we ordinarily perceive is tenuous and temporary and therefore, again like a mirage, its "reality" is only of an illusory sort that ceases entirely when reality-itself, the truth, is seen.

This may not, so far, be persuasive, but it is not difficult to follow. We may, however, have more trouble when Shankara goes farther and indicates that while nothing can be said that does justice to the "really real" (since our language arises as a product of our experience of illusion), we can at least affirm that it is non-dual, without distinctions, separations, or otherness: "When once the apparent reality of the world has been set aside, all that remains is pure Being. The seers of Brahman realize that non-dual Reality."[22]

The boy gazing at the river has, in fact, been imposing on the truth (which is both himself and the river without being in any real sense divided) false images of self and other. If he becomes enlightened, he will cease to see the river or to be aware of himself as a boy; and when he subsequently becomes aware again of river and boy he will know that their separate individual existences are only apparent, for the reality to which he awakened in his moment of enlightenment can have no divisions, no "breaks" or separate identities to split it into fragments. While the experience of perfect enlightened awareness persists (and for no one does that experience last long in its full intensity), the boy will be pure consciousness without any object—contentless awareness in fact, for to be aware *of* anything would be to introduce a second, an "other" or an object, and thus to divide the simple into the diverse. Even self-consciousness must be lost in such a moment of enlightenment, for it objectifies the self and places it within awareness as an apparent other.

Shankara is saying, then, that the experience—reported by some mystics—of a great moment when awareness of distinctions is lost is an experience of reality. Or, rather, it is simply reality itself, beyond all experiencing of anything. It is what truly *is* when all illusion and error have disappeared. This state of objectless awareness would be as "natural" to us as awareness itself if we were not conditioned to see instead a false world of manyness.

Imagine a man sitting in a room into which no scent, no sound can come. Let him be free of any awareness of taste, and let him be sitting so comfortably that he is unconscious of touching anything. He has only one sense in operation: vision. This he disciplines until it sees only one object (perhaps a candle flame). For a long time he practices having that single image in his mind. Then he closes his eyes and retains in his mind only the remembered image of the flame. No sense is in operation, but his mind is filled with just one idea. Then imagine that he manages to obliterate that one idea. What remains? Not unconsciousness, but consciousness that is pure, that "contains" nothing, that is contaminated by no content. In this state of pure consciousness the man would be perfectly tranquil, since he has removed from awareness all that could disturb or threaten; he would have surmounted even such disturbances as joy. He would be in perfect peace. And the state of enlightenment which is, at the same time, the state of *perfect Being being perfect* is at least akin to the state to which Shankara directs us. Behind the rush of images—the illusions and shadows that we mistakenly take to be a world—reality is undisturbed, perfect, and objectless awareness. It bears our experience of distress and conflict, but it is not really touched or broken by it. To cultivate the experience in which myself and my entire world have disappeared in pure stillness is to have moved out of error and to *be* the truth—not merely to know it.'

This is a very attractive vision. Those who believe it believe that reality really holds no terrors, for what can afflict him who knows himself to be all that is? It is a strange tiger that would bite itself! Thus, in the Bhagavad-Gita the god Krishna can advise the reluctant warrior Arjuna to go forth into battle even if it means killing his own kinsmen, for in truth who can possibly die? And who can possibly kill? Reality does not destroy reality, so all our suffering and conflict exist only on the plane of illusion. Again, I have no need to feel inferior to anyone, for who else is there? In final truth I am reality itself, perfection, and only the habit of falsehood mixed with the poisons of egotism leads me to see myself otherwise.

Yet in an unfortunately inexplicable way illusion exists and causes us to suffer. I think of myself as a real person, as having objects to love, hate, or fear, as having a self to protect. I am assailed by virulent viruses within and treacherous associates without. I am real, singular, and vulnerable. How does this strange error of judgment arise, and how may I transcend it?

There are mythological attempts to account for the world-illusion in Indian religious thought, but ultimately it is not to be explained. Stories abound of the great Lord (Ishvara), who by his power to deceive creatively produces a world, much as a magician might bring a rabbit from a hat. But this is for the simple mind whose questions can be satisfied with such answers. The more sophisticated inquirer must be content to know that while he *has* a question about the arising of error, he is still caught in the error, and when he is finally liberated from it, it will not exist to be inquired about.

The heart of our problem is that we impose upon the infinite reality the images of finitude, one of which is our impression of self. The cure for the problem, then, is the experience of *in*finitude, if we may have it, and there are disciplines which will lead our subjectivity in that direction. Shankara attempts, in his philosophy, to justify the belief that the subjective experience of infinitude is the truth, but it is the experience itself that is of supreme importance, for he who has it *is* the truth and needs no more philosophy.

The philosophical justification of Shankara's nondualism would require more pages than we can devote to it here, but important in it is the observation that everything within empirical experience is transitory. This means (in accordance with Shankara's presuppositions) that nothing empirical is "real"—at best it is a sort of "real appearance" like a mirage. We all know what it is like to mistake one thing for another—to see a coil of rope and instantly react in fright because we think it is a snake. Closer inspection shows us our error, and the first judgment we had made is abandoned in favor of one with more support in fact. We laugh at our fear and cheerfully kick the "snake," which we now see to be only a rope after all. But he who transcends the world-illusion goes a step farther and knows that his "rope" is also a transient vision, and it vanishes utterly when his awareness is perfectly fulfilled in the indivisible reality which admits of no "real" fragmentation into snakes and ropes and other things. It is this reality alone which has permanence. Here the parade of decay and diminishment which is the history of material things has no place—their very transitoriness is the demonstration of their final lack of reality—and what remains, the real itself, is beyond matter, beyond change, beyond any category we could apply to it. It simply *is.* Its name is Brahman or, if we are thinking of it as our own authentic inner reality, Atman.

This, then, is a way of viewing the universe that solves the problem of accounting for the relation of subject (a knower) and object (the thing known) by saying that neither is real at the empirical or worldly level, but that both are absorbed in a reality, Brahman, which is simultaneously knower, known, and act of knowing. That is to say, we have here a non-dualism of a cosmic Subject. In the ultimate mystical experience we reach the point where that cosmic Subject alone is, for we have systematically driven our own subjectivity into itself by the elimination of all objects from awareness.

Shankara leaves us with the Alone, Brahman, which is perfect being, perfect contentless consciousness, perfect bliss. It has no boundaries, for it is All; it has no divisions, for it is "not-two." If it were otherwise, it would be less than real, for the real is, by Shankara's definition, unchanging and eternal, and these aspects require also that it be unlimited and undivided. In Brahman the object has vanished; all relationships have vanished. There is peace.

The Buddha lived thirteen centuries before Shankara. However, the Buddha had attacked in his own day (sixth century B.C.) some of the things Shankara was later (eighth century A.D.) to try to reaffirm. Let us, then, look at a few criticisms of the position we have outlined, first from the perspective of Theravada Buddhism and then from our own point of view.

The first criticism of the Buddha, as this is recorded in the scripture of the Theravada tradition, is that the mystical state on which most Indian religious cults rest so heavily is not finally a reliable disclosure of truth. As one who had traveled that road to its end, the Buddha speaks to us of the highest "spiritual" conditions as being attainments of mere tranquillity and nothing more. In the Majjhima Nikaya there is a "Discourse on Expunging," in which he lists the various traditional stages of mystical trance and points out that many men regard each of them as representing the elimination of all error and the attainment of truth, but of the very last and highest of them he says:

> This situation occurs, Cunda, when some monk here, by wholly transcending the plane of infinite consciousness, thinking: "There is no-thing," may enter on and abide in the plane of neither-perception-nor-non-perception. It may occur to him: "I fare along by expunging" [i.e., I have expunged error and all illusion]. But these, Cunda, are not called "expungings" in the discipline of an ariyan [i.e., the Buddhist discipline]; these are called "abidings that are peaceful" in the discipline for an ariyan.[23]

As a contemporary Theravadin has written, "all these mystic states, according to the Buddha, are mind-created, mind-produced, conditioned *(samkhata)*. They have nothing to do with Reality, Truth, Nirvana."[24]

This is a serious challenge indeed, for it assails the dogmatic affirmation that mystical attainment is an entering into truth. But so far it does so only by offering a contrary dogma: that a subjective state is, after all, only a subjective state and that, however authoritative it may seem to the subject himself, it carries no intrinsic guarantee of value.

In the second place, the Buddha had vigorously attacked the idea, so important to Shankara, of Brahman-Atman. Shankara thought that the reality of the unchanging, eternal "Not-two" was self-evident, but the Buddha did not find it so.

Brahman, or Atman, is beyond categories, for it is beyond our limited rational understanding. But we can say that Brahman is *saccidānanda*, which means "perfect being," "consciousness," "bliss." It is eternal, undecaying, unchanging. Now, the Buddha habitually responded to the dogma of Brahman by asking for the grounds upon which such a belief is held. Is there anything at all ever experienced or known by us that has these qualities? If not, we surely have no justification in inventing the idea of Brahman.

If someone replies to this Buddhistic objection that the mystic's highest state is Brahman-itself, the Buddha points out that even the mystic does not remain in the "highest" state, but always returns to the world of ordinary perception again (although his perceiving may be colored by his recollection of the mystical condition). This means that while the mystic's highest state may be bliss, he has no reason to say it has anything to do with eternity. Even a Shankara returns from the paradise of non-discrimination to write books! No state of mind or matter is ever known as eternally unchanging and perfect, and if it were, it would not report itself (for that would represent change). Where, then, do we find Brahman?

A common response to the sort of critique outlined above is that although a mystic's great moments of intuition may be transient, they are nevertheless a foretaste and an unquestionable guarantee of a permanent condition to be attained after death. It is then that the petty empirical self will dissolve and the great cosmic Self alone will remain, eternally triumphant and eternally perfect. Such a view the Buddha regarded as mere wishful thinking. Having boldly exposed the brevity of everything we know, including the subjective impression of infinity, the Buddha found no place in which an elusive Brahman might hide its nest.

> But, monks, if neither Self nor anything belonging to Self [i.e., to the inner, permanent, enduring, and unchanging essence] can be found, the opinion that "The world is Atman, and after dying I shall be permanent, lasting, eternal, unchanging forever," is utterly ridiculous.[25]

Some modern Indian philosophers, notably Radhakrishnan, have argued that it is only the small, petty ego that the Buddha is denying, but I must agree with Walpola Rahula and other Theravadins that the Buddha's attack goes much farther than that. It is aimed at nothing less than the Atman or Brahman—the singular, indivisible reality—itself.[26]

Another of the Buddha's criticisms is implicit in his

own constructive philosophy. There is a more rational way of understanding our human experience than non-dualism offers, and it, too, gives rise to spiritual disciplines that lead to the attainment of a state of enlightenment and peace. If you affirm the sole reality of an eternally indivisible and non-dual Brahman, the world must eventually be seen as less than real. But then what is it? If it is illusion, whose illusion is it? Some of Shankara's critics were later to press this point: if the illusion of a world is Brahman's, there is surely no hope for us. If the illusion of a world is Brahman itself, how can Brahman also be perfect knowledge (since a Vedantic principle is that ignorance or error cannot coexist with true knowledge)? But if the illusion is not Brahman's, whose can it be? Not "mine," since "I" and "mine" are part of the illusion! No; if you begin with a prejudice that reality is not-two, you end in incoherence, inconsistency, or confusion, unable to account for the very problem your philosophy and religion attempted to overcome. But if you take the opposite pole of experience as your starting point, things become much clearer. We shall see in a moment the Buddha's alternative, but first let us raise a few additional objections to Shankara's system of ideas.

Shankara and his followers in the present day have always argued that, even if their position is philosophically vulnerable (since non-dualism is impossible to save from incoherence when our language is inescapably dualistic, requiring subject and predicate for any meaningful formulation), their *experience* of the "Not-two" which is All is irrefutable and conclusive to those who have had it. Shankara has argued that every experience and perception we have can be challenged by a conflicting one, but that the experience of cosmic unity cannot be so challenged, since it is the one condition in which there is no otherness, no ground on which a challenging alternative might stand: where all is "not-two," it is obvious that there can be no argument, since it takes two to make a quarrel.

To this position one might respond that the "spiritual" disciplines by which one narrows attention and finally eliminates all objects are, after all, essentially systems of repression. One has simply eliminated the object from awareness by refusing to entertain it there, and if one tries to justify this rationally, one does so not only on a wrong premise (that of the ultimacy or decisiveness of private, subjective experience) but by a process which in itself denies one's conclusion, since a rational argument is inherently dualistic, proceeding from premise to conclusion.

A non-dualistic experience of pure consciousness (Brahman), then, can be believed to offer an entry into truth only by an act of faith in which one is prepared to deny arbitrarily the final reality of the most frequent and ordinarily most important facts of everyday life—including especially personal relationship. Such a faith must lead to a distorted response to the world. To put the matter more plainly, if you begin with the assumption that the thinker, or subject, is the ground of reality and then proceed to drive yourself more deeply into your own subjectivity, it is inevitable that the world of objects is at last lost and at best seems insubstantial and apparent. But has one not merely surrendered the capacity for objective sensitivity? One may then be tranquil and feel secure, but at the expense of failing to do justice to objectivity. If this state of pure subjectivity could be indefinitely sustained, would we have reached a spiritual pinnacle or merely a condition of extreme psychopathological withdrawal? The legendary Zen monk Bodhidharma may have spent nine years staring at a wall in rapt contemplation of truth and—at moments, at least—aware of himself as the One. But to outsiders he was still just one among many, aloof and silent, to be sure, but available to be kicked, patted, and fed—decidedly an "other." Who is correct, Bodhidharma or those on whom he depended for his continuing life? I submit that the monk's subjective experience is more easily explained within a concept of objectivity than the objective world around him is explained by his subjective non-dualism.

The most obvious differences between a non-dualism such as Shankara's and a system that allows at least a dependent reality to the world, such as Christianity, may be seen easily if we make the following comparative summary:

SHANKARA	CHRISTIANITY
The world is appearance, not reality. Its origin and apparent existence are finally inexplicable. It, and our awareness of it, are to be transcended.	The world is dependently real and arises (by whatever process) as the creative intention of God, the Ground and Power of existence. It is to be enjoyed, suffered, and perfected.
The ultimate character of reality is a kind of impersonal consciousness that dissolves all distinctions.	The ultimate character of the God in whom all reality is grounded is love that creates and values distinctions.
Salvation is from error and is by a knowing in which	Salvation is the acceptance of a cosmic love that

SHANKARA (cont'd)	CHRISTIANITY (cont'd)
my individuality is overcome.	requires that I accept my own limited individuality within God.
Love is a means, among others, for the transcending of self and the losing of a preoccupation with identity in myself and others.	Love entails the effort to fulfill my own integrity (i.e., love of myself) and an equal concern for the integrity and well-being of others (i.e., love of neighbor).
The self is to be overcome by an effort that loses it.	The self is subordinated to the supreme Other and to the service of existential others, resulting in the loss of pathological (sinful) self-interest.
Pride is abandoned as we transcend by strenuous effort the sense of self-awareness.	The effort to transcend self-concern is seen as the fruit and fuel of pride. Arrogance can be defeated only in the humility that accepts an unearned, free forgiveness from God.

All this may be condensed into the observation that, from a Christian perspective, Shankara's metaphysics illegitimately turns its back on particularity. Its abandonment of the world in the moment of highest mystical intuition is not the gaining of liberation, as it may seem to be, but is the loss of destiny, for it is in the world and as a part of the world that the human adventure is to find whatever fulfillment it can have.

Indeed, another critical observation that might be

made is that the abandoned world of objects inevitably returns to haunt him who has rejected it. We have observed that even Shankara wrote books to justify his conviction that All is not-two: but if his conclusion is true, for whom did he write books? One may well feel that attempts to escape this question by talking about "two levels of truth or experience" are sophistries hopelessly entangled in the dualism they are trying to avoid.

Finally, a criticism might be framed concerning Shankara's idea of the primacy of contentless consciousness. Consciousness is never known by us to arise without content, for we are awakened to awareness by an object that we perceive by one of our senses. One may, then, ask how consciousness ever first arose if there was no object to awaken it. And even if it is possible for us today to return to a state wherein we no longer have consciousness *of* something, is this not the psychological equivalent of a "return to the womb" and a rejection of the fact, demand, and gift of existence?

After all, a consciousness that is contentless must "know" nothing—and it cannot even know that it knows nothing. It is, thus, non-cognitive and can legitimately give rise to nothing but silence.

Theravada Buddhism

There are two ways of regarding the long stretch of sand at Waikiki: one can think of it as a beach, or as an infinite number of grains of sand. The Vedantist, on the one hand, regards reality as a Whole—in our metaphor he sees the beach in its unitary entirety. The Theravadin, on the other hand, regards the "beach" as a concept rather than a reality, for it is a name for the coming together of a sufficient number of individual grains.

Reality is in these single grains, and the name we give
to their aggregation ("beach") is only a convenient
label.

The Buddha challenged many prevailing modes of
thought in India, and he did so with devastating lucid-
ity. Where, he asked, do we find evidence for that indivisible Whole which some men name Brahman or Atman? Where do we actually find the qualities which
Brahman is said to have? Where is there, in other
words, a single instance of *permanence?* Or who has
found unchanging *bliss?* Who can honestly say that
they have actually known an eternity of *pure consciousness?* If we critically search for these things, we find all
claims for their reality eroding before our eyes. Of
course the mystic knows a trance state beyond awareness of any thing or awareness of no thing: but such a
state is merely mind-produced and, like every other
state of mind, comes to an end eventually. To maintain
that it signals a prospect of eternity is to clutch desper-
ately at straws and to fly in the face of the evidence. Of
course the mystic knows bliss. But he returns again to
the world of pain, and even if his view of that world has
now been so modified that he feels above the pain, still
he has returned. And the indivisible Atman can simply
not be found anywhere at all, except in the deluded
imagination of those who have allowed their wishes to
interpret for them their mystical experience.

What is actually seen by him who has his eyes open
is that all is flux. Nowhere is there "Being-itself," but
everywhere Becoming-itself is disclosed. The old man
looks back over his life and remembers its stages. Does
he realize that the boy whose experience he remembers is not, strictly speaking, the same entity as the old
man who remembers? They share a stream of con-

nected moments, no doubt, but in the years of his life everything has changed. The atoms of his body have been displaced by others over and over again, and every moment is a genuinely new one. This, indeed, is the root of our only hope of salvation, for where static Being with its persisting "perfection" makes the hope of improvement futile, a concept of ceaseless Becoming with nothing static or enduring in it means that the process can be guided to some desired end.

Existence, then, for the Buddhist, is largely characterized by three words: *kṣanika* ("momentary"), *svalaksana* ("unique") and *dharmamātra* ("particularized," almost in the sense of "atomic"). As T. R. V. Murti aptly says, "it is discontinuous, discrete, and devoid of complexity."[27]

The human being is, then, not a solid entity but a flow that is constituted by a series of infinitely small and brief time-particles called *dharmas.* These *dharmas* collectively produce all our mental states, all our physical parts, and whatever objects we may be relating to at any moment, physically or mentally. And there is no substratum bearing this flux; there is no enduring Self or soul that is the "real" within the passing. I am a flux, a process, a sequence—and nothing more. Neither within me nor beyond me is that eternal Self called Atman.

Thus—and this is the important thing for us to grasp at present—there is awareness, but no subject having it; there is thought, but no thinker; there is action, but no actor. The subject has here been abandoned in favor of a flow of moment-entities or moment-forces *(dharmas).* Curiously enough, this idea, if we can accept it, brings peace as surely as does the Atman idea. To believe that my true essence is the eternal Brahman and therefore needs no defending is comforting, but to believe that there is no true essence in me to defend is also comforting. I can then enjoy what is to be enjoyed in the passing flux, becoming attached to nothing and no one, and discover the perfect tranquillity of a leaf unselfconsciously drifting in the stream. Those, on the other hand, who choose to cling to the sense of personal identity or even of cosmic Selfhood are, I may believe, imprisoned in a hopeless pursuit of fulfillment. Those who

> regard consciousness as having a Self, regard consciousness as being in the Self or the Self as being in consciousness . . . run and revolve round and round from body to body, from feeling to feeling, from perception to perception, from activities to activities, from consciousness to consciousness. . . . They are not released therefrom, they are not released from rebirth, from old age and decay, from sorrow and grief, from woe, lamentation and despair.[28]

We are each, then, merely a combination of *dharmas* —entities or forces that are themselves new every minute. Nothing passes on from one moment to another, but each *dharma*, having flashed into existence, passes instantly out of existence again, to be replaced by another. Thus, far from being or having an immortal soul, we represent a continuum of physical and mental moments, and every moment is conditioned in form and content by the irrevocable law of cause and effect that is called *karma*. This means that every willed action has its consequence, and that consequence constitutes in part the form and content of a new moment in the continuum of which I am a present instant.

It is significant that when Buddhists wished to speak of an individual they often chose to call him *santāna*,

which means literally a "stream," a flow of intercon-
nected *dharmas* rather than a substantial or enduring
entity. That is to say, the river is an aggregation of
drops, which are themselves new every moment; there
is no enduring essence of "riverhood," and the word
"river" is merely a convenient label for a continuing
flow in which nothing endures.

This concept of constant flux with nothing bearing it
or enduring within it is difficult for most of us to take
seriously, yet it is neither implausible nor unattractive
in the light of everyday experience. We know that our
bodies are constantly being renewed, and we know,
too, that our states of mind are always changing. How
long can we hold a stable idea or mental image? We live
daily in the experience of change, yet we persuade
ourselves that stability is the norm and that change is
the exception. Is it not reasonable instead to say that it
is apparent stability that needs explaining? Someone
will say that we can cultivate the capacity to hold a
single thought in our mind for longer than a moment,
so something clearly remains stable as the basis of that
sort of activity. But the Buddhist points to an electric
light, which seems to emit a constant glow but which
may be understood rather as a very rapidly flowing
series of light impulses. Again, a cinema seems to present us with simple continuity of motion on the screen,
but we know that we are actually seeing a series of
photographic images replacing each other so rapidly
that they present the illusion of uninterrupted continuity. So life is the rapid displacement of one momentary
entity or force by another, and stability even of the
highest mystic states is really only an illusion. Every
moment's particle of consciousness is new. It may contain a memory, but that memory-bearing consciousness

is a new entity with every second, conditioned into its present form and content by its relation to the last awareness-particle, but new nevertheless.

After all, where do we have experience of anything that *has* the awareness and itself endures? In Britain, David Hume also concluded that we never experience ourselves as experiencers but only as the content of experience itself. I may say, "I know I am writing this." But I do not know and cannot objectify the "I" that knows the "I" that is writing! My self-awareness is always awareness of an object, and there is no reason to argue for a subject bearing the awareness since we can never be aware of that subject.

Theravada's criticism of Descartes would therefore be that his statement "I think, therefore I am" simply went seriously beyond the empirical data available. He had experienced "thinking," but he could not experience the thinker. So why postulate a thinker at all? Why not say simply, "Thinking is; therefore, thinking is!" It is the only statement we can safely make.

There is, then, no demonstrable "knower" present in my simplest and most individual existence; much less is there reason to argue for a cosmic Self or Atman.

According to Buddhism, the Absolute Truth is that there is nothing absolute in the world, that everything is relative, conditioned and impermanent, and that there is no unchanging, everlasting, absolute substance like self, soul or Atman within or without.[29]

Against the more or less idealistic non-dualism of Shankara, then, we have here a pluralism of moment-entities or forces *(dharmas)* that are real even though impermanent. What does this mean for the question of subject and object?

To put the matter plainly, the subject has here been abandoned in favor of unenduring moments of consciousness. *Subjectivity* is, but it requires no subject. It is by learning to let subjectivity be unpossessed by an illusion of "self" that we allow peace to become its character. Indeed, a major Theravadin discipline called "mindfulness" requires me to objectify all my feelings and thought processes so that I learn to see at last that they are simple entities with natural sequences and not the products or possessions of an "I." I must objectify my "self" into oblivion. The eminent Russian scholar T. Stcherbatsky has said it very well:

> In a system which denies the existence of a personality, splits everything into a plurality of separate elements, and admits of no real interaction between them, there is no possibility of distinguishing between an external and an internal world. The latter does not exist, all elements are quite equally real towards one another.[30]

Here every threat to my happiness and security has been as surely overcome as it was in Vedanta, but now it is not by the dismissal of the objective world but by the abandonment of the reality of the ground of subjectivity. In Vedanta we have as real only the great cosmic Subject, which gathers all empirical subjectivity and objectivity into itself so that they finally vanish. In Theravada we have as real only a flow of real but generally highly transient entities or forces, a flow that is endless and beginningless, but from which the pain of self-consciousness may be exorcised by the abandonment of belief in either the empirical or the cosmic Subject.

What objections may be made to this Theravadin position, first from a Vedantic point of view?

In the first place, Theravada's denial of the Atman as our true essence is unconvincing. Not only have the great and ancient seers of India declared its reality, but it is surely self-evident (say the Vedantins) that a world of purely contingent and temporary realities is not self-explanatory. Theravada's ontology, its theory of being, is quite incoherent without some enduring substratum to *bear* the flow of things and provide a ground for experienced continuity. Nagarjuna, a Buddhist, but of a rival tradition that believed in an Absolute Reality in some respects similar to Vedanta's Brahman (and in other respects different), probably had Theravadins in mind when he said:

> It is on account of emptiness [the Absolute itself, not to be confused with nothingness] that all things are possible, and without emptiness all things will come to naught. Those who deny emptiness and find fault with it are like a horseman who forgets he is on horseback.[31]

Shankara himself is amazed that anyone should deny the reality of the Atman:

> O you ignorant one! Why do you assert the blissful, ever-existent Ātman, which resides in your own body and is (evidently) different from it, which is known as Purusha and is established (by the Sruti as identical with Brahman), to be absolutely non-existent?[32]

Of course the Atman cannot be discovered by empirical inquiry. Of course the "I" that says *"I* know that I am writing this" eludes discovery: the eye cannot see the eye, yet the eye most certainly is, and without it there would be no seeing at all. Similarly the Atman, the enduring spirit within, is necessary if patterns of meaning are to appear in our experiences. Is the idea of a "stream" *(santāna)* that, although entirely new every moment, bears memories, fulfills anticipations, and experiences continuity, easier to accept than a timeless spirit that is the ground of all our experience?

Indeed, Shankara is convinced that the very fact, obvious to all, that through all the changes from infancy to old age, through misery to joy, from physical fitness to decrepitude, there runs a thread of continuing self-recognition is evidence enough of Atman. In my dotage I chuckle and tell interminable stories about my misadventures as a child. Is it not clear that this continuity through change deserves a name? Its name is *spirit,* and the deepest reality of spirit is Atman. "It is a fact of direct experience," says Shankara, "that the 'I' is without any change, whereas the body is always undergoing changes."[33]

Again, does the Theravada pluralism adequately account for such stability as there obviously is in the world? In order for a theory of discrete, momentary entities *(dharmas)* to explain the regularities of nature and experience, one must entrust to some force (e.g., *karma*) a very high responsibility indeed. If *karma* does bring about consistent consequences, one must ask how it can do so while remaining quite "other" than the *dharmas,* which remain, in turn, utterly "other" than each other. Surely it is more plausible to hold to an essence that permeates all and contains all and is being expressed always. *Karma* either becomes suspiciously like Brahman, the engulfing One, after all—or it is hard to see how it can effect such continuity and stability as we perceive in the world.

But even if Theravada can account for stability, can it account for motion? Here is an even more serious charge, since it certainly seems at first glance as if the

Buddhists were almost preoccupied with motion. If they cannot account for *this*, they are surely in great difficulty. Yet, motion seems to be excluded by the theory of infinitely brief *dharmas*. These are radically separate from each other and immeasurably transient. How then can there be motion? As Stcherbatsky remarks, echoing a long line of Indian critics (Vedantist and other): "A really existing object, i.e., an element [*dharma*] cannot move, because it disappears as soon as it appears, there is no time for it to move."[34]

This is an especially serious charge because with the denial of the possibility of motion comes a threat to the possibility of causality, and Theravada has tried to account for the universe as a network of causality. But if the *dharmas* are utterly separate and individual, and if they endure so briefly, it is obvious that one does not move another and none of them produces another. Production as well as movement, then, is inexplicable.

Vedantists, and even Buddhists of other schools, in this way found the Theravada explaining of life to be no explanation at all. Its gaps were so vast and serious that, in the opinion of Theravada's rivals, even if its disciplines—"mindfulness" and the rest—lead to peace, they are founded upon wrong principles.

Western critics have also tended to agree with most of what has been critically said above and to develop some points in accordance with their own perspectives. Thus, as an example, we may take the question of cognition. Does Theravada offer a reasonable account of how we perceive and come to know things?

In the Theravadin explanation of perception we find that elements *(dharmas)* of color, of vision-experience, and of pure awareness are all involved in "seeing" a color. But if these *dharmas* are really separate entities, how can they explain the unity of a perceptual experience in the absence of a *perceiver* who is himself other than, but a gatherer and coordinator of, the *dharmas?* In other words, in a system that believes in no subject and holds that a visual experience is a composite of quite independent elements, how is consistently ordered experience to be explained? Why, for instance, do we not find ourselves with an awareness of the vision-experience instead of an awareness of color?

Stcherbatsky, speaking specifically of another but related Buddhist school, the Sarvastivadins, says correctly that the answer is that although the elements do not invade each other and coalesce, yet "there is between two of them—consciousness and object—a special relation which might be termed 'co-ordination' *(sarupya)*, a relation which makes it possible that the complex phenomenon—the resulting cognition—is a cognition of color and not of the visual sense."[35] Stcherbatsky then aptly points out that this is no answer at all but a confession of ignorance. It is to say that a cognition of color occurs because it occurs; that the relation between *dharmas* is "special" because it *must* be special to account for what happens; but we are not told *how* it can be so.

From a Macmurrayan point of view, Theravada fails because in seeking to keep some contact with empirical reality it lacks the intellectual premise and the viewing point from which a true statement might be made. It may attempt to qualify dramatically the importance of the subject (empirical or cosmic), but it has no recourse except to the language of subjectivity, and its final defense of its thesis is appeal to a subjective experience induced by certain disciplines of mind and body. In short, it is as firmly locked up in the prison of the subjective as is Vedanta—and philosophy in general, Eastern or Western.

It is now time for us to essay a critique of both Vedanta and Theravada and to place as an option beside them the understanding of reality afforded by a dialogical Christian theology.

We have seen that Shankara chooses a form of pure and absolute subjectivism in which empirical subject and object are both subsumed; Theravada, on the other hand, chooses objectivity as its theme, eliminating the subject in favor of discrete ontological entities, some of which have the character and perform the functions of subjectivity. It may be contended that neither of these solutions to the tension of subject-object relations will suffice, for neither is able to fulfill itself. One may indeed attain the experience of pure subjectivity, but the objective world *is still there,* and it even returns eventually to intrude upon one's awareness; we must either make concessions to that objective world which we have attempted to deny, or we shall die. Again, one may imagine a state of pure objectivity, but the objective world eventually fails to account satisfactorily for subjective experience. In "mindfulness" I may objectify all my mental and emotional processes, see their arising and falling as caused by this or that, without any reference to a true subject ("I"), but there is always that subject which is doing the objectifying!

Both Vedanta and Theravada argue that their final experience (of Brahman or of Nirvana) is beyond the reach of doubt, but in the question of the significance of doubt another major break with dialogical Christianity emerges. Doubt may certainly end if the capacity for doubting is abandoned or its tools are lost, and Vedanta loses the awareness of otherness or objectivity that is indispensable to doubt. If one's awareness is, by elimination of all objects, unitary, there is no doubt possible. But this by no means "proves" the truthfulness of implications drawn from the experience. Similarly, Theravada overcomes doubt by achieving the loss of subject and thus also abandoning the possibility of a confrontation of subject and object in which doubt might flourish. But for the Christian, this lack of the capacity to doubt only indicates a weakness in personhood, for one of the polarities proper to personal awareness, "faith-doubt," has been allowed to disintegrate and thus faith itself, no longer aware of itself as *faith*, is distorted. Where doubt is not the formative pole within faith itself, what is left is not true faith or true knowing, but merely a truncated sensitivity in serious peril of becoming fanaticism.

The distortion of the faith-doubt relation is, thus, an inevitable consequence of the destruction of the subject-object wholeness with which our conscious life is ordinarily replete. It is achieved through a sacrifice of reality, and—even though its reward is tranquillity and a sense of undivided wholeness that seems to carry its own authentication (since doubt is abolished!)—the Christian may regard it as costing too much and demanding the wrong sort of payment. Our human awareness begins with a subject's birth in the encounter with an object, and it may be doubted whether a solution that fails to do justice to both entities and their relation can do justice to the strange and wonderful human adventure at all.

Again, both the Vedantic and the Theravadin approaches to life seem, theoretically at least, to dismiss too arbitrarily the seriousness of relationship, especially of personal relations between two subjects. One may still speak of love and compassion and so on, but unless the inviolable otherness of my partner is acknowledged, he is in danger of being merely a convenient tool for the development of my own character: I love him because in so doing I move forward spiritually, but I do not love him for his own sake. This is to reduce the other to a means to my own ends, and even if I speak, perhaps, of overcoming selfishness through my compassion, the very intention of using compassion to serve a purpose of my own is subtly self-centered. Nothing, indeed, is so flattering to the ego than the successful struggle to demolish the ego! And nothing leads us more cruelly to ignore the real claims of others than our treating them with love in order to perfect ourselves.

On the other hand, even if we accept the authentic otherness of our friends, relationship becomes inexplicable unless we see that otherness as somehow contained within a continuity which is its ground. Only when the continuity between persons and the discontinuity that guarantees the inviolable authenticity of each person are both integrated into our way of seeing things can we overcome some kind of depersonalizing imbalance. Perhaps the current faddishness of such martial arts as karate or the inclusive kung fu may offer some material illustrative of what I mean.

The philosophy behind much that goes by the name kung fu is, I gather, a form of Chinese non-dualism associated with the very ancient Taoism indigenous to that land. According to this, I may come to know that I cannot really be hurt because there is no authentic separation between myself and the world and, as a snake does not strike at itself (at least as a rule), so the great One (Tao) does not destroy itself. But this also implies that I can really *do* no injury to another, for there is no one who is really other.

The foregoing is, of course, an oversimplification, but it will suffice for our present purpose. On the ground of the assumption of the essential oneness of all things there is developed a system of personal combat of great efficiency and subtlety, the aim of which is to enable the perfector to know himself in command in every situation. He ought to be pacifistic as a matter of course, but he can afford to be so now because he knows himself competent to defend himself against any enemy. He can be gracious precisely because he has almost demolished the reality of those to whom he is gracious.

The cross, the central symbol of Christianity, points to a much more radical non-aggressiveness: the willingness to be a victim, to be vulnerable. There is here the act of taking the other so seriously that one knows at once that he can hurt and be hurt, and a willingness, as the ultimate attitude of healing in a world of terrible estrangements, to leave oneself defenseless as an act of trust which knows it will be betrayed but cannot modify itself and remain the gesture adequate to generate the possibility of real healing.

In other words, love and respect for persons requires a trust of them which we know will be violated sooner or later, but which we will not cancel by preparations to counter their aggression. This is a hard doctrine, demanding far more courage than is needed to be pacifistic when we know we could triumph. Indeed, it is a doctrine that few persons, Christian or otherwise, are ever likely to fulfill perfectly in the living of their lives. But its difficulty does not allow the Christian to abandon it, for even its imperfect performance is some proclamation of the worth and integrity of persons.

Where the Self is really All (Brahman), or where there are no selves, there must be a tendency to dismiss too lightly the value of the individual person and the alarming wonder of our elusive authenticities.

One school of Buddhist thought—the Madhyamika—launched a powerful critique of the formulations of all its rivals and reached the conclusion that language is incapable of expressing the truth about reality. Words about Brahman or Atman were no better than formulas based on *dharmas,* for the Real eludes all conceptualizing. With this opinion Christianity may heartily agree, and some of the most important Christian statements about God have been entirely negative—specifying what may *not* be said about him rather than what may. Yet there are two things that move the Christian to speak. One is the need to say something that will prepare us for an appropriate rather than an inappropriate response to God and his creation, and the other is the conviction that a unique and unrepeatable Self-disclosure of the divine has occurred toward which words may direct our attention, even if they cannot do justice to it.

The disclosure-event is, of course, that personal presence which we call the "Christ." We have already said something about this, but let us now make a brief additional statement in order to throw dialogical Christianity into clear relief against the background established in this chapter.

Both Theravada Buddhism and Advaita Vedanta see self-conscious finitude as a problem. For the former, suffering arises because in a pluralistic and highly transient stream of elements there arises a self-consciousness that longs to preserve itself. For Vedanta, suffering arises because self-consciousness arises to create an illusory separation between us as apparent individuals and our true being, which is non-dual Reality. Both

Theravada and Vedanta see the longing for personal existence as the root of our troubles, Theravada because it leads us to fear the inescapable flux that is worldly transience, and Vedanta because it precludes our realization of ourselves as the impersonal and indivisible "Not-two."

Against these attitudes, Christianity celebrates our finitude and sees our problem as sometimes the mistaken desire to be infinite and sometimes contentment with being nothing—or, at any rate, less than we are destined to be. God is indeed the realm and power to be of whatever is, and every proposition about him must fail: Christianity may be as insistent upon that as Vedanta. When Moses seeks to know the name of God, he hears: "I am! Tell them 'I am' sent you."[36] Yet particularity is also a fact to be neither ignored nor transcended, for it is not a "fall" from some perfect condition but the way that God wills to be. In particularity there is a richness that no unity without it could accomplish, a richness expressed not only in love and in the joy we establish for each other but also in the mystery we are for each other, a mystery whose depth we may ignore and whose surface we may devour, but which can be entirely lost only in blindness and infatuation. Not only is God the power of my being and the inclusive reality in which my reality moves; he is also my *limit.* And we are limits of a lesser sort to each other, yet these limits are embraced in the One who is God.

Thus, not simple identity and not simple particularity and pluralism, but identity in particularity and particularity in identity constitute the world as Christianity sees it. This is the fountain of our wonder and dismay. This is why love and sorrow, but never perfect isolation or perfect unity, can lead us to the truth that transcends One or Many. This is why the "peace" of the Christian is not a peace which "the world" can give,[37] for it is neither the tranquillity of non-discrimination nor the resignation that follows from an abandonment of personal selfhood.

All this the Christian learns from what he holds to be the supreme dialogical event in this world's history. If, as is probable, there is sentient life on other planets, that life may have a different word to meet a different need. But among us the "Word" in which the Christian finds truth breaking itself open for him is the Christ. Why do we call this a dialogical event?

Christ is neither disembodied deity nor a simple humanity but, as we have seen, he is divinity wearing the structural contraplete of humanity. In him we find the concrete instance of divinity-humanity, of eternity-temporality, and of infinity-particularity. We see in him that to seek consistency in our logic by the denial of any of these contrapletes is to achieve *in*completion and to pay too high a price for logic. This "Word" is as beginningless as God, as the first chapter of the Fourth Gospel claims, yet it is also as local, material, and particular as an atom. "He has appeared once and for all at the climax of history," as Heb. 9:26 (NEB) puts it. Here, then, in living presence, is the unique exemplar of the form of personal logic, the spiritual embracing the material in order that both together may be shown to be holy.

If the Christ "came" many times, he would not be the Christ, for he would have destroyed the dialogical Word by eliminating the contraplete of unique singularity that his once-for-all appearance expresses. If, as the docetists imagined, he had come among us with merely the appearance of humanity, he would similarly have broken the Word of contrapletion, for spirit alone would have been uttered. But we who see the Christ and—with an astonished cry—discover our moment of awakening, our Zen-like flash of illumination, are led thereafter to affirm the seriousness of the One and the many, spirit and matter, heaven and history, for in reality-itself these are not poles in tension but contrapletes in mutuality. Because other contrapletes include destiny and freedom, there is always the risk of disruption and the evils of the world must be faced as real. But even those evils speak to us now of the inexpressible fullness of reality.

Death itself is seen, in Christ, to be the contraplete of life. Martin Heidegger has affirmed that it is our having to die that makes our living valuable, and this is true for the Christian in a sense that extends beyond Heidegger's. Death is the pole that shapes life by marking its value and raising it to consciousness of itself as the possibility of finite and therefore selective value. But when life itself becomes disordered and alienated from its ground in God, death becomes disordered too, and sometimes the contrapletes are reversed, so that the suffering in life is felt to raise into prominence the value and preferability of death; this means that suicide becomes an aberrant salvation.

The worldling is inclined to become lost in a forest of particularity that alarms and dismays him and, sometimes, leads him to fly into the womb of a cosmic Oneness. The "spiritual" person longs to be wrapped in that oneness and finds it relatively easy to discount the importance or reality of the world. The Christian accepts alike the burden and the joy of particular existence without confusion, for he knows that it is within God but is, as God's intended mode of being, entirely serious and not to be forsaken.

The great Madhyamika Buddhist, Nagarjuna, was

convinced that fondness for things—attachment—was the root of all human suffering and led to reincarnated life after life of futile questing for satisfaction. So he exploited a logic which discredited every possible statement one might make about virtually anything and by means of that logic tried to show the "emptiness" of everything in heaven or earth. Money, fame, security; truth itself, and even final spiritual liberation (Nirvana) he showed to be empty—to be ungraspable. For he who longed for salvation was bound to the endless wheel of rebirth as surely as he who longed for wealth, since *any* form of attachment, longing for *anything*, was the cause of our imprisonment in life.

Nagarjuna was, therefore, more radical than either Advaita Vedanta or Theravada Buddhism in his eroding of all modes of expression and all grounds of hope. But this program of denial he undertook not as a cynic or skeptic, but because of his belief that deliverance, peace, and escape could be had only when one clung to nothing whatever.

I have always been an admirer of Nagarjuna. His is the consummation of all those lines of reasoning which are based on the conviction that suffering is unrelievedly an evil to be escaped, and that we must begin our quest for what is real upon the basis of the self as subject. The true scandal of Christianity is its claim that however ungraspable or inexpressible the ultimately real may be, it is not utterly in discontinuity with the world, so that whatever is in the world is, in some way, its manifestation. Thus even suffering must somehow—at least potentially—administer the presence of the divine; and the network of relations between persons and between personal and impersonal entities also expresses him who is the power of all being and becoming. So a monopolar logic must always fail to find the truth, and a "personal" or bipolar logic may only waveringly point toward it. Yet the critical thing, the staggering thing, is that God himself has disclosed himself in a Word/Act that in one dazzling moment of history has revealed the dynamic contrapletal character of reality and has demonstrated that true personal existence is relational, founded upon neither subject alone nor object alone, but upon the mystery of their engagement. Thus salvation is not *from* the world, but *for* and *in* the world. It is salvation not to the magnificent aloneness of pure consciousness, but to the cosmic mutuality of pure love.

All this is implied by the God-man, the Christ. Yet all this, like every attempt to verbalize the truth about God, is inadequate and, alas, undoubtedly misleading. For the Christ is not only a revelation-event. When we begin to turn from the direct contemplation of him to speak *about* him, we disclose that he is also the concealment of God, for the limitless grandeur of the Creator cannot be encapsulated in a moment without concealment. Thus the Christ is a revelation-event inwardly structured by concealing flesh. This is the enigma which reduces all our theology to necessary impotence and requires that again and again the theologian turn from words to the Word itself, the Christ, that he may stand speechless before the perfect comprehensiveness of that event.

And as he stands there, if the memory should arise of his words, in all their printed majesty, he must find himself with no recourse but laughter.

Notes

1. Carter Dickson, *The Magic Lantern Murders* (London: William Heinemann, Ltd., 1973), p. vii.

2. Joseph Sittler, *Essays on Nature and Grace* (Fortress Press, 1972), p. 96.

3. Eliot Deutsch, *Advaita Vedānta: A Philosophical Reconstruction* (East-West Center Press, 1969), p. 44.

4. Robert C. Whittemore, "Jonathan Edwards and the Theology of the Sixth Way," *Church History*, Vol. XXXV, No. 1 (March 1966), pp. 60–75. Diagrams reprinted by permission of *Church History*.

5. René Descartes, "Meditation II," *The Philosophical Works of Descartes*, tr. by E. Haldane and G. Ross (London: Cambridge University Press, 1931), p. 192.

6. John Macmurray, *The Self as Agent*, The Form of the Personal, Vol. I (Harper & Brothers, 1957), p. 29. For *Persons in Relation*, see below, n. 12.

7. *Ibid.*, p. 80.

8. *Ibid.*

9. *Ibid.*, p. 107.

10. *Ibid.*, p. 109.

11. Lal Mani Joshi, *Studies in the Buddhistic Culture of India During the 7th and 8th Centuries A.D.* (Delhi: Motilal Banarsidass, 1967), p. 228.

12. John Macmurray, *Persons in Relation*, The Form of the Personal, Vol. II (Harper & Brothers, 1961), p. 48.

13. *Ibid.*, p. 90.

14. John Macmurray, *The Self as Agent*, p. 97.

15. *Ibid.*

16. John Wright Buckham, "Contrapletion: The Values of Synthetic Dialectic," *The Personalist*, Vol. XXVI (1945), pp. 355–366.

17. *Ibid.*, p. 355.

18. Erich Fromm, *The Art of Loving* (Harper & Brothers, 1956), p. 26.

19. Peter Taylor Forsyth, *Positive Preaching and the Modern Mind* (Independent Press, Ltd., 1949), pp. 10–11.

20. H. Richard Niebuhr *et al.*, *The Purpose of the Church and Its Ministry* (Harper & Brothers, 1956), p. 45.

21. Mircea Eliade, *The Sacred and the Profane*, tr. by Willard B. Trask (Harcourt, Brace and Company, Inc., 1959).

22. Acharya Sankara, *The Quintessence of Vedanta*, tr. by Swami Tattwananda (Kalady, Kerala, India: Sri Ramakrishna Advaita Ashrama, 1970), p. 128.

23. Majjhima Nikaya I. 41–42.

24. Walpola Rahula, *What the Buddha Taught* (Grove Press, Inc., 1962), p. 68.

25. Majjhima Nikaya I. 138.

26. Cf. Rahula, *What the Buddha Taught*, p. 59.

27. T. R. V. Murti, *The Central Philosophy of Buddhism: A Study of the Madhyamika System* (London: George Allen & Unwin, Ltd., 1960), p. 10.

28. Samyutta Nikaya 22. 99.

29. Rahula, *What the Buddha Taught*, p. 39.

30. T. Stcherbatsky, *The Central Conception of Buddhism* (Delhi: Motilal Banarsidass, 1970), p. 58.

31. Lucien Stryk (ed.), *World of the Buddha* (Anchor Books, 1969), p. 286.

32. Acharya Sankara, *Aparokshanubhuti*, tr. by Swami Vimuktananda (Calcutta: Advaita Ashrama, 1966), p. 19.

33. *Ibid.*

34. Stcherbatsky, *The Central Conception of Buddhism* (Delhi: Motilal Banarsidass, 1970), p. 39.

35. *Ibid.*, p. 56.

36. Ex. 3:14.

37. John 14:27.